BENGAL
The Unique State

About the Authors

Prof. J.N. Nanda, with a string of academic distinctions including two earned doctorates, multitude of awards from the IBC and American Biography Association, and other national and international awards, is a distinguished scientist, thinker and writer. He has represented India abroad many times. He has summarized his all embracing philosophy and religion as New Mahayana in which all 'isms' co-exist. Among his scientific contributions, mention can be made of his new light on the earth's internal structure, the origin of the moon and the origin of earth's magnetism etc. He has travelled practically in all continents and studied many languages. Besides his scientific books and publications, mention may be made of his book *Science and Technology in India's Transformation*, released by the President of India at the Rashtrapati Bhawan in 1986. Other important books are *Conflicts and Co-existence—India, Glimpses of Indian History and Culture, Co-operative Development of the Resources of the Sea—India and Religion and Philosophy for Modern Youth.*

BENGAL
The Unique State

J.N. Nanda

CONCEPT PUBLISHING COMPANY, NEW DELHI-110059

Cataloging in Publication Data—DK
Courtesy: D.K. Agencies (P) Ltd. <docinfo@dkagencies.com>

Nanda, J. N. (Jatinder Nath), 1920-
Bengal : the unique state / J.N. Nanda.
p. cm.
Includes bibliographical references (p.
Includes index.
ISBN 8180691497

1. Bengal (India)—History. I. Title.

DDC 954.14 21

ISBN: 81-8069-149-7

First Published 2005

Published and Printed by
Ashok Kumar Mittal
Concept Publishing Company,
A/15-16, Commercial Block, Mohan Garden,
New Delhi-110059 (INDIA)

Phones : 25351460, 25351794
Fax : 091-11-25357103
Email : publishing@conceptpub.com

Dr. A.R. KIDWAI
Governor of Haryana
and
Formerly Governor of Bihar
and West Bengal
and M.P. (Rajya Sabha)
Former Member of Parliament
(Rajya Sabha)

सत्यमेव जयते

Foreword

In his book "Uniqueness of Bengal among the Indian States" Prof. J.N. Nanda, who is an eminent Physicist, has critically analyzed the various historical events which led to Bengal's political, cultural and religious developments over the centuries. In his approach Prof. Nanda has been very objective and discerning—the traits of a true Historian.

According to Prof. Nanda, Bengal has a uniqueness in the Indian national matrix. Thus the concept of hereditary monarchy or the dynastic rule was first opposed by the people of Bengal. The seeds of democracy were first sown in Bengal when the people democratically elected a leader to save them from internal chaos and the external attacks from Tibet and from the East. Thus Gopala, the strong ruler of Gauda, was so elected and Pala dynasty followed.

Even in trade and commerce Bengal had long flourishing trade relations with Burma (Myanmar), Java, Cambodia, etc. Buddhism and Hinduism spread extensively, historical relics of which are seen in plenty. The Temple of Angkor Vat shows the influence of art and architecture of Bengal.

According to Prof. Nanda, a joint identity was given to the Hindus and Muslims of Bengal through the Bengali language which developed as one distinct from Sanskrit, though it had its roots in Sanskrit. It helped the growth of a common culture.

The author has remarked that an essential ingredient of the integrated Indianness of Bengal is a contribution of Sufism. In fact, Bengal became the main Sufi centre in India. The goals of Hindu and Sufi Mysticism were identical and paths similar. In the medieval period Bhakti Cult and Vaishnavism were the manifestations of this.

Vivekananda and Ramakrishna of the 19th Century were influenced by liberal humanism preached by Sufi saints.

In Bengal, people began to identify Shiva with Akbar, Kartik with Qazi, Goddess Chandi with Eve (Amma Hava). King Hussain Shah, a patron of art and literature was popular with the Vaishnavas of Bengal who regarded him as an incarnation of Lord Krishna. Even in the Bengali Katha of Lord Satyanarayana, incarnation of Lord Vishnu, Fakirs have been idolized. Lord Satyanarayana has been identified with Lord Satya Pir. Thus even before the concept of Din-Ilahi by Akbar to bring about a synthesis of the two dominant religions, namely, Hinduism and Islam, a serious attempt had been made in Bengal to develop a harmonious relationship among the different religions—a practice which has been handed down even to this day. Thus communal riots witnessed in several parts of India or the recent mayhem in Gujarat cannot be dreamt of in Bengal.

In the 19th Century, renaissance and national consciousness dawned in Bengal. At the forefront were Raja Ram Mohun Roy and Prince Dwarka Nath Tagore. Brahmo Samaj was established bringing in reformist ideas in Hindu faith and belief.

In the 19th Century, art and literature greatly flourished in Bengal. Ishwar Chandra Vidyasagar started writing Bengali prose, Bankim Chandra Chatterjee wrote 'Vande Mataram' which is one of the national anthems now. He wrote many novels which inspired nationalist ideas. Michael Madhusudhan Datta introduced Miltonian sonnet in Bengali Poetry. He wrote "Meghnad Badh Kavya" based on the mythological story of Ramayana, but unlike the epic Ramayana version popular in North India. Michael projected the positive sides (virtues) of the demon Ravana and his son Meghnad.

According to Prof. Nanda, Bengali intellectuals were in the forefront at revival of arts and crafts, industry, etc. The reason is obvious. The British Rule had started in Bengal. After winning the battle of Plassey in 1757, the East India Company established its foothold in Calcutta and started spreading its tentacles in the West and South of India. Naturally the people of Bengal first enjoyed the advantages of British Rule. They reaped the benefits of western education while the rest of India were still smouldering under oppressive native rule.

There was little participation of the people of Bengal in the Sepoy

Mutiny in 1857. Like the people of Punjab, Bengalis also did not join the uprising for two reasons. First, they were satisfied with the orderly British Administration and did not want to go back to the situation of anarchy and chaos prevalent in the native administration. Second, in the Sepoy Mutiny they did not see the fulfilment of the aspirations of the common people. They saw the mutiny only as an outburst of some native rulers who were being gradually deprived of their authority by the British.

Instances can be multiplied. However, all the facts stated above, are recorded events of history. They establish the main theme of the book, namely "Uniqueness of Bengal among the Indian States". Prof. Nanda has brought out this aspect convincingly. He has demonstrated that over the centuries the people of Bengal have played a path-breaking role in promoting social and cultural cohesiveness transcending the barriers of casteism and religion and have been in the forefront of scholarship and learning extending the frontiers of knowledge. In my opinion this is the rich tradition and heritage of Bengal which should continue in the years to come.

I would, therefore, strongly commend this book to the readers for their serious study.

(A.R. Kidwai)

Preface

Indian history and culture is multi-dimensional. Bengal has all kinds of priority. I count many Bengalis among my friends and colleagues. Throughout the last century Bengal spread like the sky over the rest of the country. The Bengalis ran the country while serving the British colonial sahibs. They also spearheaded the fight for freedom forestalling many of the tools of struggle for the freedom movement and produced self-sacrificing band of freedom fighters who refused to wage only a non-violent struggle. They were vindicated when the mahatma gave the call of "Do or Die" to the youth of India and justified even a violent struggle to end injustice. I recall the all embracing personality of my friend Prof. S.D. Chatterjee who had in his lonely pursuit of science at Calcutta discovered the nuclear fission much before anyone else in the world. He was not given any attention. Only much later the American Society of Engineers elected him as an honorary fellow of their society. He was invited by the Carnegie Institution of Washington to repair some of their equipments in 1949 where I met him and we remained lifelong friends. I often stayed with him at Ballygunge Place in Calcutta. He was a committed bachelor and later bequeathed all his wealth to Chatterjee Research Foundation. He introduced me to the swami-in-charge of the Ramakrishna Mission and many other eminent Bengali scientists and artists. Another close friend of mine was Prof. P.K. Bhattacharya who besides being a prominent geophysicist was a dancer and sang Tagore's songs beautifully. He was given a special invitation to visit many institutions in the Soviet Union in order to present finer points of Indian dance and music. It seems to be a Bengali trait to carry a superior intellect but express their achievements in low key. They achieve but remain modest. The Ramakrishna Mission, a Bengali institution reflects Bengali character fully of love and self-less activity and full commitment to Indianness.

What Indian secularism or the Indianness can grow into is best shown in Bengal. In the rest of north India, it was bedevilled by successful Muslim aggression and the Indian assimilation and integration efforts were less successful. In Bengal half the Muslim rulers were either native or at loggerheads with the Delhi imperialists. The joint culture prevailed where all religions and modes of life were thoroughly coexisting. By seeking their fortunes in the Indian Union the Muslims of Bengal have demonstrated their trust, which has grown in time, of the Hindus. There are weighty inter-communal contacts in Bengal than in Punjab or Delhi for example. The Bengali is evolving continuously and being Buddhist, Hindu (Saivite or Vaishnavite), Jain or Tantric, yoga addict or democratic traditionalist or terrorist revolutionary, capitalist-*cum*-communist etc. are all temporary phases in Bengali evolution. Bengal might yet make the core of global culture. Bengali Muslims are the majority in Bangladesh which is at present standing on the razor's edge of communal division and harmony. We are certain that it will seek its destiny in harmony which will have far reaching benefits to the global struggle against the Islamic imperialism based on terrorism. Study of the history of modern Bengal and Bangladesh fills all Indians with hope of a glorious future.

India is indebted to Bengal in many ways. Gangaridi, a pre-Mauryan ruler of Bengal had such an awe-inspiring army, that Alexander's soldiers lost heart and refused to cross the Beas river and go further east. Bengal kept up its trade with foreign countries all along. It was rich in the production and export of grain, salt, fruit, liquors and wines, precious metals and ornaments besides the output of its handlooms in silk and cotton. Europe referred to Bengal as the richest country to trade with. The riches of Bengal can best be sensed from its ruined cities and many monuments scattered all over the country, e.g., the ruins of Gauda, Tamlok, Lakshman-Vati, Paundravardhan, Vardhman, Samatata, Chittagaon, Satgaon, Rudranagar, Bishnupur, etc.

The author is indebted to Dr. S.K. Zaheer for going over the manuscript and for valuable suggestions. The help of the Khuda Bakhsh Oriental Public Library at Patna and especially of the Director, Dr. Mohammed Z. Ansari is gratefully acknowledged. I had a memorable stay at Calcutta Raj Bhavan for over a week as guest of H.E. the Governor Dr. A.R. Kidwai and I visited, as his guest, the remnants of most European settlements in South Bengal as well as the exquisite terracotta studded temples of Bishnupur.

Contents

1

Introduction

While Indian and Asian thinking is open-ended, Arab and European mind lay stress on classification and specialisation. They always classified Indian religion and philosophy as nebulous and unbounded. A Jew is of chosen race and must rule. A Muslim is granted the teaching directly given by Allah to the prophet. A Christian has only to firmly accept Christ as the only begotten Son of God and he is assured of heaven in the next world and supremacy in this world. When exposed to religious argumentation common in India from ancient times, they tended to compartmentalise Indians as Hindus, Buddhists, Jains, etc. and present day categories include Sikhs, tribals and *dalits*. The masses of India were only Indians and had faith in humanism (Manav dharma), i.e. they were Sanatanists and the same person could be struggling at various rungs of the religious and philosophical ladder. If an invading band came across a Buddhist king, they imagined they were in the Buddhist period of Indian history and were equally sure of seeing a Hindu revival when the ruler they came across was worshipper of old deities. The Indians or Bengalis were just plain Indian or Bengali and were living their life of free thinking and free worship of the deity they chose or which was then popular. Periodical fairs were held regularly exalting sometimes one and sometimes the other deity. A fair in honour of Siva could also play up Dharma, a Buddhist deity or a fair in honour of Chandi could slide into the worship of Hariti and so on. This is still going on in Bengal. If the area teems with fishermen, the local deity of fishermen will hold court for visiting deities of the jungle or the supreme from the hills.

The situation changed when Islam crept in. At first Muslims were given the same attention as received by other Indian visitors. Muslim derveshes and fakirs were honoured the same way as the Hindu, Buddhist or Jain ascetics and monks but later the aggressive stance of Muslim captains brought a reaction of silent withdrawal and slowly pushing them to unimportant isolation. The moment lid of oppression and Afghan-Mughal neglect was removed, the Hindu mind and their devotion to humanism and reason again prevailed in the form of Vaishnavism exalting a life of service, love and devotion to Krishna. Soon after this, the ruling English company administered justice without bias against any Indian religion or caste, the Hindu renaissance began in earnest. Freedom from British rule was taken in its stride. Netaji has shown a glimpse of what integration Indians are capable of. The day is not far when Bengal and India can demonstrate a unity in diversity which is the ultimate goal for the world ensuring secular democracy and coexistence of economic and social disciplines of all kinds under the UN umbrella and policing of the world against terrorists, narcotic smugglers, pirates, etc. Much hope is centred on modern advances in medicine, management and science and technology as well as in economics and philosophy.

We will not subdivide Bengal history into Hindu, Buddhist or Muslim, etc. periods but treat it as a flow past ascetics and derveshes (holy wanderers), captains and kings, suffering humanity and slow dawning of sense in the social and political leaders with sudden upsurge of reactionary upheavals and imperialist machinations. The slide back of secular outlook in Bangladesh and the reaction citadel in the Muslim *madrassas* (religious schools) that abound in the subcontinent have to be overcome primarily by the efforts of Indian Muslims and learned theologians working in the footsteps of Maulana Azad and Khan Abdul Gaffar Khan.

1.1 Bengal's Uniqueness

In all the Indian states, Bengal is the most populated. Its geography covers the entire range from mountains to seaboard. Ancient cities and modern mining towns are there. It is home of the famous Calcutta University established in the 19th century and of Shanti-Niketan, an experiment of new education by Rabindranath Tagore Nobel Laureate. In Bengal there is the headquarters of the Ramakrishna Mission, the Hindu missionary society set-up by Vivekananda. Bengal has been the cradle of the freedom movement in India. Bengal has produced great minds and great leaders in the last century like Tagore, S.N. Bose (Physicist), Shri Aurobindo (modern Indian Yoga fame) and Swami Vivekananda besides political leader of the calibre of Subhas Chandra Bose (of INA fame) and outstanding artists and film makers and story tellers like Satyajit Ray as well as industrialists and entrepreneurs in every field, etc., etc. The West Bengal state of India is the state where Hindus and Muslims had practically integrated to the disappointment of the British imperialists. The masses jointly participate in religious *pujas* and processions. Bengal has own dress and manners and many jointly celebrated festivals and bathing fairs; such participation of Muslims was criticised by Jehadists.

Bengal has been the home of Indian revolutionaries much ahead of Punjab and Maharashtra. They are approaching the ideal of a continuous revolution first described by Jai Prakash and are experimenting with democratic communism! Bengal is well known for its Dacca muslin, Bankura horse, Bishnupur terracotta, and Baluchari saris. Bengal has the oldest Christian church in North India. Bengal has been in maritime touch with civilization both of the east and the west. On account of helpful sea currents in the Bay of Bengal, most sea-borne trade of India passed through Bengal. It had good river communications. Bengal was the colonizing state for emigration of Indians to the east upto Japan. Bengali baboos provided the Indian backbone to the British colonial empire and also its eventual liquidation. The Bengal revolutionaries took to the violent liquidation of traitors and particularly oppressive British agents. The Indian renaissance flowered first in Bengal. The Bengali intelligentsia spread all over India and participated in the country's awakening.

A Bengali would burst into song and dance at the slightest occasion. Bengal scholars have made a name for themselves all over the world for culture and application. Afghans and Moghuls became friendly in Bengal. Bengal impressed all by its Vaishnava doctrines of love and fellowship.

Kolkata mornings are indeed memorable. There is strange mingling of afterglow and moon-light in autumn. The winter trees including the leafless pipal uplift the soul. Lotus in ponds, the birds and the fish are ever reminding one of nature at its best. The grand banyan tree in the botanical garden of Kolkata is a spectacle in itself.

There is uniqueness also in the ruins of Bengal and its arts and crafts discussed separately.

1.2 Hindu Society of Bengal

The Hindu society of Bengal as in the rest of country has been evolving continuously. In spite of poor communications, there was always movement of ideas and people from one place to the other particularly since people enjoyed going on pilgrimages and attending fairs. The worship of Siva and devi has been there since distant past. Varanasi and Ganga were held as sacred city and river respectively. The rivers of Bengal provided, for the larger part of the year communication channels. There were many scared bathing sites from Varanasi to Ganga-sagar and townships developed at nodal points. Brahmans were given a higher status in society and expected to live high moral life devoted to teaching and thinking or to guide the people in sacred tasks and rituals. After fair advance had been made in the Harrapan culture at the mouth of the river Sind, or in Vedic composition and gurukul system of oral transfer of knowledge from the guru to the resident disciples, or the tribes in the jungles had evolved the sacred rites of propitiation of their devis and devatas, the travel on invitation of the Brahmans increased. North Indian Brahmans also could carry arms and were in the forefront of Hindu intrusion in new areas covered by jungles and marshes and infiltrate through better knowledge or better arms. The tribal wizards and representatives lived in amity with Brahmans treating them as respected guests and learning proper ways of worship of local deities. Sivalings were established all over Bengal. Similar consideration was also available in Bengal to Muslim fakirs and divines when they landed there from Arabia or Iran. During Afghan hegemony in Bengal the immigrant Muslims from north India were usually professional soldiers or Muslim preachers who were ready to dispute with monks of various Hindu orders and often had the upper hand especially when they competed in magical powers as the Muslim divines were also adepts in Yoga and meditation. The Bengali society looked at all as gentlemen and expected civilized behaviour from strangers and suffered as other Hindu societies when confronted with dismal standards of dealing of others like the Muslim aggressors out to despoil the Kafirs or the Europeans holding themselves morally superior to heathens how-so-ever unethical be their own behaviour. It is to the credit of the Bengali Hindu that he had already established his superior culture with respect to the people of the East. The Hindus of the rest of the country have taken to do this with respect to Europe almost a millenium and that too with assistance from European learning, historical research and favourable accidents of fortune after an interlude of slavery and enforced introspection.

Going back to the first millennium of the Christian era, many teachers and preachers took the long road to the east *via* the sea ports of Bengal and Orissa. They travelled on Bengali trading vessels and were taking with them the Bengal products as well as learning imparted in Bengal including Magadha and Orissa. The eleventh century saw more graceful forms in Hindu sculpture and arts. Many illuminated manuscripts from the Pala days have come to light. There are engraved drawings on copper plates of Brahmanical, Buddhist and Tantric subjects. Hinduism had continued to be inclusive of all streams mixing and evolving together: the primitive tribes: Kola, Saraba, Pulindas, Hadis Dom, Chandala and Nishads, Santhals, and freedom loving fishermen or sailors and boatmen living in their boats at various anchorages, river and sea ports. Bengal armies and communications employed thousands of elephants which had scared the Greek invaders of India and would continue to be the nemesis of all invaders. The Hindus wrote new Puranas to suit the internal conditions. As an example a Brahman of 30 years age could get engaged and eventually marry a girl of only ten years of age. This freed the high caste soldiers for longish duty at borders and long training in arms with assurance that they could safely postpone looking for a wife or setting down in peaceful enjoyment later. The Hindu concepts of transmigration of the everlasting soul and rebirth had become common knowledge very early. Sanskrit contributed mightily to the development of the Bengali language which had its own literature only with the popularisation of the Vaishnava cult of Hinduism by Jaideva, Vidyapati, Chaitanya and Chandidas. Bengali literature was earlier in the form of *padavalis, dohas* and ballads.

High caste Hindus could be teachers, soldiers, traders or agriculturists. The professions avoided by Brahmans were medicine or painting. Due to local conditions, the Puranas compiled in Bengal allowed Brahmans to eat meat and fish particularly white fish. Devals (Brahmans of lower order) could also be astrologers, while in the rest of the country astrology was bread and butter for the Brahmans. Karna caste (non-Brahman) was engaged as scribes while a local Samariti groups them with barbers and potters. One is surprised at the low status accorded to potters when they were the creators of wealth and artistic expression. The potters and artists of India have emerged from obscurity regarding social and financial status only after current independence and the eye-opening advances in Europe and in East Asia. The credit goes again to the high caste artists of Bengal of the 20th century. Nagar Brahmans were immigrants from the Punjab, and Kamboj Brahmans from U.P. Many Bengal Brahmans trace their ancestory to Vedic Brahmans specially invited by King Sasank or who came in the wake of Kalinga intrusions and south Indian expeditions into Bengal often for the sole purpose of pilgrimage to the Ganga. They took the Ganges water from Bengal all the way to the south to sanctify the pilgrim spots or temples flourishing there. Later south Indian rivers like Godavari and Cauvery have begun to command the same sanctity. Radhiya and Varendri Brahmans of the older Bengal kingdoms claim descent from the mythical times of Adisura when pristine Hinduism spread again into Bengal in the 9th century after the decline of popular support of Buddhism and Jainism.

Many illuminated manuscripts from the Pala days have come to light. There are Brahmanical subjects engraved in copper plate drawings of various pantheons, the style being classical (linear). The primitive tribes were having own co-existence. Most Bengalis were deemed as Kshatriyas who could intermarry with immigrant Brahmans. Pala kings upheld the orthodox caste system. *Brihad Puran* represents the then Bengal conditions. Due to local compulsions, Brahmans (usually warriors) could marry child brides of eight and settle down in married life after their initial military tenure. Brahmans, could also be in the agriculture profession. The barred professions to Brahmans were the practice of medicine or painting. Many Brahmans continued to trace their ancestory from the original band imported by King Sasank to tone up his army and the upkeep of Vedic worship. Bengal had distinct art and literature from the rest of the country.

In India castes were determined by birth though in principle these are determined by the aptitudes that a human being is endowed with at birth. Only in Bengal repeated attempts were made to tally facts with theory. Raja Kshiti Sena divided Radhiya Bangali Brahmans into three grades based on their *gunas* or inherent qualities: Mukhya Kulina, Gauna Kulina or Shrotiya Kulina. According to Vachaspati, king Vallal Sena founded Kulinism based on assessed number of virtues visible in the conduct of a Brahman but with time, the various categories also became status from birth as demanded by the karma and re-birth theory. Dhivre, Kaivarta (fishermen) and Mahashyas of East Bengal gave the local aristocracy to Sena kings who improved their social status. The eleventh century saw an upsurge in Hinduism when popular Vaishnavism spread equal status in worship through Harinam Sankirtan. Adivasi castes like Doms, Chandals and Savara took to dancing and singing professions and acquired an honoured status. The worship of devi through often a mixture of Hindu, Muslim and Buddhist practices was common in popular fairs. Tantra brought all castes together in the worship of divine mother as Kali further glorified by Shri Ramakrishna an ordinary worshipper of Kali who has become the pinnacle of Sanatanist thinking of modern times along with Mahatma Gandhi and the Nobel Laureate Tagore.

High castes avoided mushrooms, onions and garlic, but partook of liquors and wines and even exported these. Imbibing of wine was part of Tantric ritual. Paharpur sculptures show the usual dress and ornaments worn by men or women. Long tresses of men were allowed loose while the women tied these in a knot. People walked barefoot and so did their gods. Religion became degraded due to uncontrolled spread of Tantra and dependence on magic. Even human sacrifice became a thing of godliness. It is the practice of Tantra that could not stand the inroads of Islam whether in east Bengal or in Indonesia. The simpler religions of Bhakti could do this with greater success.

1.3 Hindus and Buddhists of Bengal

History books make a distinction of Hindu and Buddhist periods which is unwarranted. In Buddhist times beginning in the seventh century B.C. all Indians followed Sanatan Dharma or the ancient faith still prevailing among adivasis, i.e. worshipping a form of devi, and Siva and which is still followed by most non-Muslims of India who form the great majority. Many savants, laboured to give content to Sanatan Dharma. Vedas were composed in hoary antiquity succeeded by the Upanishads and Smaritis. Brahmans propagated the Vedic *sanskriti* (culture) supported by the popular compositions: *Ramayana* and *Mahabharata*. Around the time Upanishads were written, the world was having many religious and culture reformers and creators like Buddha and Mahavira in India, Confucius in China, Hammerabi in Mesopotamia or Socrates in Greece. There was considerable river and sea borne trade. The ideas have a way of travelling across continents. The Brahmans of India had perfected a Gurukul system of instruction and had worked for the popular support of Brahmans as possible gurus for the upbringing of their children.

While the Brahmans regarded the Vedas as the referee authority, the Buddha and Mahavira wanted the ultimate referee to be human reason. Both the Buddha and Mahavira frequently travelled in Bengal and spread their philosophies among people establishing Viharas and Sammelans. Some rulers patronized these also because of their subjects which did not mean that the state became Buddhist or Jain. Jain temples were in vogue from 6th to 8th centuries. Today one can find many ruined Buddhist Viharas and Jain temples in Bengal as well as some flourishing centres of these modes of worship.

Magadhan empires extended deep into Bengal. Most Pala rulers were Buddhist while the Sen rulers were mostly Saivite. Vaishnavism was native to Bengal following the songs and works of Jaideva, Chandidas and Shri Chaitanya. The first Muslim invasion was in 1202 A.D. There were various Delhi appointed governors of Bengal and almost continuous strife between the various Afghan and Bengal factions. Most governors would prefer to rebel and create own fiefdoms. In 15th century Ganesh a man of destiny again usurped the governorship and had a separate succession of Hindu governors independent of Delhi except that they would often agree to accept nominal suzereignty of Delhi and give some customary *nazarana* fee. In order to save their position, some even accepted to become Muslim. Many temples housed both Hindu and Buddhist gods as was prevalent all over Sanatanist India. The popular religions were Vaishnavism, folk religion summed up in Sanatan Dharma. Islam spread rapidly due to the activity of Arab traders along the Arakan coast. Many Muslim pirs and fakirs spread themselves in Bengal after the stability seen for some time after Akbar snatched Bengal with the help of Raja Man Singh and his sons. The Muslims also added many locally cherished idols and objects of reverence as mythical pirs or their relics.

An apt historical classification in Bengal would be Sanatanist or pre-Muslim, Muslim, and European capitalist/imperialist.

The word Hindu was coined much later than the supposed Hindu period of Bengal. The Buddha himself was a great Hindu who enthroned reason, logic and popular acclaim as the referee rather than the Veda, as the supreme authority. The Jains also did the same though the Buddhists as well as the Jains could glibly quote the Vedas and criticise the Vedic teaching if a criticism was possible. In the famous Buddhist Nalanda University, the Vedas as well as the Buddhist gospels were taught in the syllabus. In those days it was customary to have a guide or Guru and for the guru to have disciples. Like the modern universities in USA the student could change his academic committee chairman (or Guru) with the acceptance of the disciple by the new guide. The student remained a seeker and did not become a non-Hindu. All Buddhists who preferred Buddha's logic still were Hindus; the same holds for Jains. Same person could hold firmly to some Buddhist learning and some Vedic learning. If a local temple priest placed an additional deity outside the door, there was a good chance that the deity would enter the temple or have a separate temple of its own. Now when ruined temples and ancient mounds are unearthed, besides the depiction of possibly a main deity, many other images of major or different pantheons are unearthed from the same place. Even in most present day temples it is rare that the main deity rules in solitary splendour. The current conversion of Hindu *dalits* to Buddhism is a political gimmick, it is not even an intellectual conversion or a social uplift among fellow villagers who themselves regard the Buddha as an Avatar of Vishnu like Rama or Krishna. The popular Siva Bhakti and Siva worship that is most indigenous to greater part of India continued to flourish. It is well known that Hindu religion travelled eastwards from Bengal which was the centre of Indian trade along with coastal Orissa. Even now one can see right in front of the royal Buddha temple at Bangkok a Sivaling in regular worship.

Popular worship often determined the religious inclination of the lord or the zamindar of the place and not the *sanad* or certificate of authority he got from an emperor in Magadha, Kannauj, Gauda, Delhi or London. Bengal intellectuals in fact have determined the content of modern Hinduism to which all Indian thinking has advanced from ancient Hinduism. The thinkers of Indian religions are for a modern version of their religions in tune with needs and gifts of the modern age, i.e. free of superstition, reactionary traditions, bondage of women, and they favour equal human rights and democracy as well as the acceptance of the scientific approach and total system analysis. The basic socialist and communist ambitions are contained in the neo-capitalist welfare state. Bengal has also been experimenting with the apparatus of a pseudo communist state and is again reverting slowly to the mainstream managerial efficiency and planned development. Bangladesh is still poised on the razor's edge between ethnic cleansing and downright theocratic state ignoring scientific advances or the role of the mass of the poor population who see the economic upsurge of the more modern states.

In Bengal (geographic area of East and West Bengal, Bihar, parts of Orissa, Assam, Manipur and Arakan) it was seldom that there was a rule of a single king. Whole of India from times immemorial was ruled by many kings in different parts. The society was mostly tribal or feudal with fealty to the tribal chief or local king. The sway of gods extended over many kingdoms and was often the main uniting factor among subjects of different kingdoms or old republics where there would be an elected chief. The Hindu or, more correctly the Sanatanist pantheon is ever expanding and has absorbed many tribal deities as well as Buddhist ones. The Hindus have extended the worship of Buddhist relics and stupas to the worship of relics or graves of Muslim pirs and fakirs and keep insisting that God is the same of all the faiths, whether, Hindu, Muslim, Christian or Sikh. The rural population of India has stuck to the popular worship of Siva, and the human avatars of Vishnu or the rivers and river or sylvan goddesses. Hinduism was always widespread in the form of crowds at fairs and at temples or on bathing festivals which occur very frequently. Every month there are one or more bathing festivals.

2

Ancient Bengal

In the *Mahabharata*, the people of eastern part of India are referred to as Paundras, Vangas or Kalingas. The region west of the Hooghly was called Radha and the region to the east was known as Vanga. The coastal region was Samatata. Coastal region south of Radha was for long a constituent of Magadha empire in the pre-Asokan period of 3rd century B.C. The major kingdoms of Bengal were Gauda, Vanga (chief city was Varendri), Samatata to the east of the Meghna river and a small state of Tamralipti near the coast. Vedic culture and superior status of the Brahmans had spread throughout the land even among the adivasis of jungles and tribal tracts. The society had upper and lower castes and various strata of people. Vishnu as a god and the Buddha as guide for action had wide acceptance. The Sanatan Dharam or the religion from ancient times recognised many gods and was not much different from Mahayana Buddhism. The philosophers and thinkers gravitated between Vedism, Buddhism and Jainism. Just like the present times, the folk venerated a mixture of gods and goddesses and were quite pragmatists in following the trendy faith and thinking. When Bengal came under the sway of the Gupta emperors and later in the empire of Maukharis of Kannauj, the popularity of Vishnu increased along with other Pauranic gods. When these empires broke up, the people of the states of Bengal suffered the consequences of anarchy in the absence of a strong kingdom and were prone to attacks of the Tibetans and the Assamese. A memorable and unique solution to their problems was spontaneously achieved by the genius of Bengal. They agreed to peacefully elect a maharaja whom they would give allegiance. Gopala, the strong man of Gauda was so elected and the famous Pala dynasty rule began in Bengal. Most Pala kings were Buddhist and Siva worship became secondary yielding the first place to Buddha and his Dharma.

King Sasanka had earlier been a devotee of Siva and other gods. The Buddhists now began to regard Sasank's reign as an anti-Buddhist time which is not borne out by facts since Sasank and most Bengal rulers would give charity to both Brahmans as well as monks of non-Vedic discipline. Brahmans well versed in Sanskrit were preferred immigrants in Bengal from ancient times till this position was also earned by Muslim derveshes and fakirs. Rampal (625–675 A.D.), the son of Gopal, subdued the Assamese by defeating the king of Kamrup. Around this time Bengali alphabet had evolved and the Bengali people could be identified as such. The alphabet and the Bengal culture were taken to Java by sailors and merchants of Bengal. The conquests of Dharama Pal reached the Punjab. Heun Tsang, the Chinese pilgrim visited Bengal around 650 A.D. He found the country prosperous and dotted with Buddhist Viharas as well as Siva, Vishnu and Jain temples. Monks and ascetics of all persuasions intermingled and jostled for followers. The seventh and the eighth centuries also saw the wide-spread use of iron. Copper was exported which brought riches to Bengal. A new era was started around 750 A.D. commemorating Pala victories in north India. Vaishnavism spread to Samatata during Khadge rule in the 7th century A.D. There was rise and fall of Jainism in the 7th and 8th centuries. Slowly by the end of Pala ascendancy in 1150 A.D. popular mood shifted from the path of the Buddha to that of Brahmanical teaching and new Puranas were composed in Bengal.

In the 5th century A.D., Brahmanical worship and rites were common all over India. Brahmans of Nagarkot flocked to Gauda. These Brahmans, besides being Vedists were also fighters and favourite professional soldiers in the Bengal armies. With the start of frequent Chalukya raids from the south and Tibetan invasions from the north, Sasank, the king of Gauda declared himself independent of Magadha rule. While the Magadha power had been committed to the spread of the Buddhist teaching, Sasank favoured Brahmanical worship. The growth of temples enshrining the Linga and the activities of roving Hindu ascetics had a new spurt. Sasank's capital was Karna-Suvarna (in the present Murshidabad district).

From ancient times Bengal had flourished trade relations with

Burma (Myanmar), Java and Cambodia. Sugar was one of the major exports. Paundra grew a sugar rich variety of sugar cane, this variety is still popular in north India under the name "Pona". Other major exports were terracotta wares, flowers made of precious stones, necklaces of pearls, bejewelled girdles and anklet bells, and stone and ivory carvings. During the Pala successors of Sasanka, Buddhist and Hindu preachers and Brahmans travelled to the east and some managed to reach China, Japan and across the Pacific to Philippines and to Mexico with the Chinese colonisers. Kumar Ghosh, a guru of the Sailendra kings of Sumatra was a Gauda. The influence of Bengal art and architecture is visible even now in the temple art and architecture of Myanmar. The 7th and the 8th centuries also saw the rise and fall of popularity of Jain philosophy among the trading classes. A new Pala era was set up from 750 A.D. from the conquests in north India by the Palas. The Pala kings ruled in Bengal from 700 A.D. to 1100 A.D. The popular mood shifted from the Jain and Buddhist disciplines to the free wheeling religion of the Puranas.

Gauda Brahmans set up a Siva sanctuary in the Mathura region of north India. King Sasank had invited some five Gauda Brahman families to Bengal who were well versed in the Vedas and Vedic rituals, in order to look after certain Vedic temples and institutions. The Sena rulers of Bengal recognized three divisions of Brahmans based on their aptitudes and later the divisions crystallised as by birth, viz. Mukhya, Gauna and Shrotiya. Later according to Vachaspati Misra, Vallabh Sena, the ruler of Bengal was the founder of Kulinism based on number of stages of erudition and virtue attained by them. Later, Kulinism got based on birth and not qualifications as originally intended. This led to popular polygamy of Kulin Brahmans. In ancient Bengal, the town people led a life of luxury. The towns were nodes of river and road communications or places of pilgrimage. The importance for pilgrims was later spread by Brahman and other priests to the nodal town and bathing places. This was their way to spread the desired worship and philosophy. Sasank died in 637 A.D. He had also come to rule Magadha who had been overlords of Bengal. He had disputed borders with Maukharis to the west. Since he was often in conflict with the Buddhist kings in the north and west. He was cautious against conspiracies of the powerful Buddhist Sangha in his own domains.

2.1 Pala and Sen Rulers

After a break in the ruling Pala dynasty when King Divya usurped the throne after killing his master, the Pala line was restored by Rampala in alliance with the Chandela king Hari Varman. The Senas and Vermans succeeded the Palas. King Dharam Pala crowned in 750 A.D., was the most famous among the Pala kings. He founded Som Vihar in the present Rajshahi district. The ruins of Saravastibhadra temple from the times of Dharam Pala with Brahmanical sculptures along with Buddha as the presiding deity have been recently unearthed. Decorated pillars with terracotta designs still stand elegantly executed. Dharam Pala also founded the Vikram-shila university at Paharpur. Inder Gupta, a Brahman of Jalalabad was appointed head of the Nalanda monastery. The Arab traveller Suleiman came to Bengal during that time.

The Senas were rulers in Radhe well before they rose to displace the Palas completely. Lakshman Sen, the son of Vijay Sena was victorious over the Assamese and Kalinga kingdoms. The son of Vijay Sena also defeated the Pala remnants in Magadha. Senas favoured the ascendancy of Brahmans and their gods. Theirs was the time of revival of Sanatanist gods and Brahmanical worship of Siva and his family of gods and goddesses. Umapati Dhara's eulogy of Sena kings has been found at Deopara. Most seats of learning were filled by Brahmans. The Senas ruled Bengal upto 1260 A.D. when Bengal was incorporated into the domains of the Sultans of Delhi. The ruins of Sonargaon represent the remains of once famous capital city Vikrampura. Many literary works were composed during the Sena period in Sanskrit. The commerce and the living standard were the envy of people far and near. There was widespread love of learning. A treatise on elephant lore and remedies of their ailments and temperament was compiled. *Samskar-Padhita* was compiled before 1200 A.D. Jemut Vahan, a Radheya Brahman was the leading authority on the Bengal School of Dharam Shastras.

During the imperial rule of Dharam Pala, many siddhas, established their centres in Bengal. This led later to the spread of Tantrism, Hindu, Buddhist or Muslim kind. Jaideva popularised the present list of ten Avataras of Vishnu so much worshipped by the Hindus. Lakshman Sen had many literary savants in his court, e.g.

Govardhan, Saran, Jaideva, Umapati and Kaviraj etc. Santi-rakshita, a Nalanda teacher composed a *Tattva Sangraha* (i.e. a compilation of philosophical issues). The Buddhist Tantra covered eleven Sadhanas; Atissa was the title used by the Tibetans for the Tantra writers of Bengal. A Bengali Siddhacharya spread Tantra in rural Bengal from where it travelled to the east Indies and led to the decay of dharma there which easily succumbed to the preachings of Islam when trade had already passed into Arab hands.

By 1000 A.D. most of the Bengali writing was in old Bengali, e.g. Chhayapada, Sri Krishna Kirtan in popular folk language. Guru Gorakhnath, the famous Nath Yogi flourished around 1150 A.D. He had a following all over north India from Jhelum to the Ganges delta. Jaideva of pre-Muslim period was matched in poetry only by Chandidas in the 15th century. Ratnakar had material for story-telling, Narrative ballads were composed during the Sena period by Gopi Chand and others. Bodhidharma regarded Bengal as outside the orbit of the Vedic culture, though the Brahmans were very much active in temples and monasteries having taken up service of various gods and goddesses worshipped by the people. Yakshagan associated with Jain cults was quite popular at various places. The cult of Vishnu had spread in Gupta times. Siva was regarded as specially accessible to outcastes and lower castes in the caste hierarchy. Siva in ling symbolic form was set up even in most inaccessible places. Siva was installed in even Buddhist and Jain places of worship since the people so preferred. Saivism in Bengal was of Pasupati sect starting from Kashmir. Siva worshippers outside India regard Patanjali as one of the devatas of the Hindu pantheon. Most Vishnu images had absorbed Mahayana features and symbols. Ram displaced the swan as Lakshmi's *vahan* showing non-Vedic influence. A stone figure of the Buddha is even now worshipped at Khulna as a Siva image. Bengal is the homeland of the Sakta cult and Devi worship in the form of Kali in various forms. Brahmanical Surya driven in chariot seems to be adapted from Rahu driven Tara in chariot. The moon god with sixteen arms was the favourite god at one time in north Bengal from where he seems to have travelled to Tibet and China. We have included some later amalgams of popular worship after the advent of Islam in this period and many graves of Muslim fakirs and *takyas* dot the countryside of Bengal and are centres of fairs and popular gatherings of pious Bengalis as in other parts of India from ancient times.

In the spread of Tantra, Hindus and Buddhists as well as Muslims converged to miracles and healing by charms and magical cures. People shifted their allegiance to popular devis and monuments irrespective of the tribal or other origin. There was a famous Tantric Siddha of Bengal with a following even in the Indian colonies in the Indian Ocean. Many medieval Vaishnava poets flourished during the late pre-Muslim period. Matsyendranath of fishermen caste composed Dohas in proto Bengali language. Santirakshita a Nalanda teacher composed *Tattva Sangrah*, an outline of philosophical problems needing close attention. The Atisa teachers of Mahayana Buddhism propagated Buddhism in Tibet. Yamban has written simple dohas in Bengali language. Putali was a Tantric sage of northern Bengal. Sidhacharya spread Tantrism in rural Bengal. In Tantrism, the people at large converged to miracle mongering and extraction of favours from the gods and the common people turned more to popular local divinities. Charanpadas and Krishna Kirtans in old Bengali were popular. Gorakhnath, Jaideva, were popular. Gopi Chand's stories and narrative ballads and other romantic legends were widely enjoyed during the Sena period.

Bodhidharma's Dharamacharita regarded Bengal as outside the orbit of Vedic culture, though the Brahmans were very much active in the worship of all deities. Siva-Linga is worshipped even in most inaccessible hamlets of Bengal since the 5th century. Siva-Linga is still enshrined outside all temples and Viharas (Hindu, Buddhist or Jain). Saivism of Bengal was of the Pashupati sect. Most Vishnu images had absorbed Mahayana features by the 10th century. Ambika and the Yakshini figures in Siva temple ruins show Buddhist interpolations. Similarly, there are Buddha images found in ruins of many temples dedicated to Brahmanical gods. Bengal is the homeland of Shakta cult. In a temple, Brahmanical Surya, in chariot was an adaptation of Tara in Rahu driven chariot. There is 16 armed Chunda in North Bengal, an adaptation from the Buddhist iconography.

Four hundred years of Pala rule was a glorious chapter in the history of Bengal. The heritage of liberty and catholicity is surviving till now. Looking at the coming medieval strife after the advent of Muslim power at Delhi, Bengal did not experience any oppression of peace loving rural population. The oppression if any was on the rich landlords and other accused of tax evasion. Hindus continued to stay and prosper in Islamic strongholds. At Delhi, Bengal was known as rebel city since every now and then there was revolt and some New Delhi approved governor or king had to struggle for his possessions certified by the imperial awards. The Hindu rulers of Assam, East Bengal and Orissa were to continue as visible centres of Hindu power until the advent of Maratha aggressors or the loyal Hindu and Muslim generals of Delhi emperors like Akbar and his couple of successors. Sharqi Sultans (Jaunpur) were new converts to Islam. The Muslim unified rule began at Lakhnauti in the 14th century which became a centre of Islamic learning. In 1244, Raja Naraindas of Jajnagar annihilated an attacking Muslim force and completely liberated Radhe, the western region of Bengal. Due to continuous fighting in most of northern India, many Muslims sought sanctuary in Bengal.

2.2 Ruins and Museums (Ancient Monuments and Stone Inscriptions)

Bengal has tropical climate, plenty of rain, shifting courses of rivers and there was for the centuries of the second millennium, a government at loggerheads with its neighbours, successors and predecessors, and even when it indulged in building new structures, it could not devote attention to preserve the rich Bengal heritage or keep existing buildings and monuments in good shape, while cities were destroyed by victorious armies or devoured by floods and clasp of jungles. The East India Company came into power in the 18th century and from start had a clear vision of eventually becoming masters of an empire in India and started looking after ancient buildings and treasures. Lord Curzon set up the Archaeological Survey of India and the Asiatic Society, based in Calcutta, promoted delving into the history of the subcontinent. The industry of Bengal builders and sculptors was so prolific that in spite of centuries of neglect and ravages of weather and floods, the remains, and idols are still being uncovered and filling the museums and private collections extant in the world. The Bengal armies at one time had ranged upto the Punjab and the rumoured size of the army of Gangaridei, the pre-Mauryan ruler of Bengal had scared away the soldiers of Alexander. Though a Gauda contingent was present to fight on the side of Chauhan in the attack on Delhi by Mohammed Gauri of Gazni, the defeat of Chauhan opened the flood gates of incursions of the Turkish tribes into India and they ranged upto Gaur in Bengal. The Afghan rulers of Delhi could not stand upto new wave of intruders and the Mughals started claiming overlordship over Bengal, thus, began wars between Afghan and Mughal factions. Gaur the capital city since ancient times now stands abandoned in ruin along the bank of the Hooghly quite close to the limits of Calcutta. Gaur was called Jannatabad or paradise city by Humayun and Akbar. It was abandoned in 1526 and the capital shifted to Rajmahal. Below is given a list of important ruins or artefact holding museums. Lakhanvati (Bakarganj) has an elegantly carved Vishnu image. Sundarbans have been depopulated by the ravages of Portuguese pirates. Ruins of the pre-Buddhist city of Paundra are in Bogra district, ruins of Devkot are at Sonitpara in Dinajpur district. Pokhran is in ruins on the south bank of the Damodar in Bankura district. The ruins of Somapura, the capital of Dharam Pala, the Pala emperor are at Paharpur in Rajshahi district. It was burnt down by a Vanga army in the 11th century. Badkanta near Comilla was the seat of kings of Samatata. Champa near Bhagalpura was the capital city of a branch of Gauda kings in the 8th century. Ruins at Sonagram represent a part of the ancient Sena capital Vikrampura.

The stone images recovered in Bengal give a complete record of Indian iconography. *Kshanik* or temporary images of gods and goddesses which are, after the annual worship, immersed in nearby river or tank must have been very ancient practice. This kept the potters busy and they could develop their craft so well. Bengal potteries have had a ready market at home as well as abroad. Terracotta decorated structures for example in Bankura district and at Bishnupur constitute a wonder of the world: complete scenes from Ramayana, Mahabharata, or Life of Krishna depicted in tiny terracotta bricks put together in a masterly design and art work, covering an entire outer wall or the facade of a temple structure inside. The terracotta section in the museum at Mahasthan is worth a visit. There is a 10th century Vishnu image of the Mahipala period at Tiperera. Most Vishnu images have absorbed Mahayana features. Lakshmi Narain relief at Basta (Assam) is a rare piece. Balrama images have the plough as well as an umbrella so important in Bengal. The foreign influence is to be seen in the Saraswati images with a ram in place of a swan. Similarly Chandi has an iguana on her pedestal. Siva with two, four, ten or twelve arms are to be seen in certain museums. The main mound at Paharpur has yielded all the navagraha deities including superb images of Chandra and Brihaspati. Ganga or Dakshin Kalika is worshipped in temples at Dinajpur. Some Vedic deities like Indra, Yama, Varuna have taken the lowly position of Dikpals, i.e. preservers of specific directional realms. There are idols of Dharma with a balance (a popular deity of the Buddhists) which is popular even now in certain tribal areas. Jain images of Rishabhdev have been discovered at Suroher (Dinajpur) belonging to the 10th century Pala period. The figures of yakshas and yakshinis, of Neminath and Ambika have been unearthed at many places. Mahasthan (ancient Pandruvardhana) has yielded a gold plaited bronze Manjushri. Rajshahi museum has many 11th century figures.

In the Sarvats-bhadra temple ruins at Paharpur, one can recognise the original from which temples in Burma and some South Asian countries were copied. This temple is of the times of Dharm Pala. It has angular projections popular in many eastern temples later, truncated pyramidal steps and horizontal lines of decoration. Dacca museum has stone pillars of Pala period including a pillar topped with a Garuda image as is the practice still in Nepal. Inscriptions in Bengali script can be seen in certain Buddhist sites of Java. The tank of Jafar Khan Ghazi at Triveni has been constructed with temple rubble. Statues showing Kushan influence are to be seen at Rajshahi museum. Pala paintings of the famous Pala school (successor to the Ajanta school) is the counterpart of the Pala and Sunga period plastic art. There is paucity of finds coming from 13th and 14th centuries since the life was visibly dislocated due to Islamic invasions and iconoclastic fervour of the invaders. The Bengalis did not use footwear and when certain idols are shown with footwear, the conclusion is a foreign influence or an idol from outside Bengal. Many idols are depicted with umbrellas as walking sticks, a usual practice in Bengal.

2.3 Some Short-Lived Dynasties

(a) *Chandra*

Lama Tarnath in his book on the history of Buddhism in India mentions that the territory of South Bengal was ruled by a line of kings with names ending in Chandra from 6th to the 8th century. A famous king was Vimal Chandra who extended his rule to Assam and Tirhut. The Eastern provinces had no kings. And the area was run by village councils. From an inscription found at Tipperera, mention is made of Ly Chandra ruling around Comilla around 1000 A.D. The Comilla ruler also annexed Harikela and Chandradvipa. Vikrampura was the capital when Shri Chandra ruled. The Chandra kingdom succumbed to the invasions of Shri Karan of the Kalchuri dynasty (1041-1270 A.D.).

(b) *Varman*

Varman dynasty succeeded the Chandra rule in East Bengal. They were descendants of Hari who dominated in Simhapura (present Singur in Hooghly district). It is suspected that Simhapura of Kalinga was their original home. Varmans of Kalinga are mentioned in the *Harivansh*. The expansion of the Varman rule in Bengal took place in the times of Jata Varman around 1075 A.D. when he married into the Kalchuri family. He was in the triangular contest between Palas, rebellious Divya and the chiefs in alliance with Karna. In an inscription found at Vikrampura, we learn that Jata Varman's able minister Bhatta Bhavadeva was from a long line of able ministers of Vanga and Radhe who had mastered many sciences. He settled many Vedic Brahmans in Bengal and facilitated their migration to many courts in the Indies. Around 740 A.D., the Varmans were feudatory to the Guptas. Their capital city in ruins is near Bagmati (Murshidabad). The prevailing philosophy was of Vajra Yan and Mantra Yan enunciated by various Siddhas. This led later to the Nath cult of North India.

(c) *Khadga*

A relatively small kingdom mentioned in ancient inscriptions is that of the Khadga dynasty (650–700 A.D.) with their capital Karnata-

Verka (Tipperera district). They were feudatory to Kamrupa and extended their rule to Java in the delta area. The Khadgas, Varmans and Chandras nibbled at the Pala empire which later passed on to the Sena rulers who were in alliance with the Kalchuris of South India.

(d) ***Sharki kings of Jaunpur (who had brief hold on Bengal)***

The Delhi emperor Feroz Shah Tughlak established a strategic military outpost at Jaunpur aiming at future control over Bengal. After his death, a favourite eunuch Malik Sarvar assumed control at Jaunpur with the title Sharki (or the king of the east). Sultan Ibrahim Shah Sharki (1401–1440) consolidated the kingdom and sent his forces to Bengal to curb Raja Ganesh who had set up a short lived Hindu dynasty there, under the advice of Sufi Khalifa Sinnani. The Sharki king was hailed as a liberator from fickle Raja Ganesh who was conspiring with many Muslim conspirators. Sharki king had a brief interlude of glory since Jaunpur was reconquered by the Delhi Sultan (Lodi) in 1584.

3

Extension of Delhi Sultanate into Bengal

3.1 Bakhtiar Khilji

Bakhtiar Khilji, a soldier of fortune of Delhi Sultans was sent with an expeditionary force by Emperor Iltmush to conquer and pacify Bengal which was considered a rebel state always in turmoil with different kings of ancient Pala dynasty or newly established Sena kingdom. He accomplished this with a handful (only twelve) of his companions. This unbelievable story has, however, a simple explanation. He told his force to follow him to the Sena capital while he went ahead on forced marches. The ruler had had advice that a great attacking host was approaching from Delhi. He took natural precaution to send his forces north for intercepting them at some distance from the capital. He was poorly served since the courtiers did not make any preparations for the defence of the capital. In this context, the wily invader entered the city with his small armed band and even reached the palace courtyard in the garb of peaceful traders. The superstitious population had also been advised by royal astrologers that the king was to suffer defeat in the forthcoming battle. The king fled with his family through the back door opening on a private boat jetty. This Khilji raid occurred in 1202 A.D. After the king had fled, the Khilji army also arrived at the gates of the town and the city surrendered without a fight in the absence of their king and the astrologers' din that the defeat was certain. Bakhtiar tried his luck by a similar attack on Kamrup and Sikkim but was crushed by them. On this defeat, he was assassinated by a colleague Ali Mardan who took control of the remnants of the force sent by Iltmush. The Sen Rajas continued to Rule in their capital cities in Bengal upto 1289 A.D. The Delhi Sultan agreed to a treaty with the Raja of Bikrampur in Bengal treating him as an equal in 1293.

In 1335, Bengal had three states under Delhi Sultan who placed his nominees as governors with seats at Satgaon, Sonargram and Lakhanauti. The Muslim period of Bengal's Kings and governors had started. It was a continuous arrival of Delhi bureaucrats and reinforcements and ignominious rebellions or assassinations with obsessive attacks on other Hindu or Muslim states in Bengal with varying fortunes till pacification and control by Akbar with his Rajput general Man Singh or his sons.

Going back to 1337 A.D., a soldier of fortune seized the city of Sonargram setting up an independent Ilyas Shahi dynasty in Bengal. In Bengal as well as the rest of India, whether the kings looked after the welfare of the subjects or not, they held on to the scriptural advice that the king must lead his armies for expansion of his kingdom. The politics in India as well as in Europe of the middle ages was only of war-lordism and feudal loyalty to the established king. There could hardly be a sustained development in such a climate further spoiled by feuds, rebellions and fights for the lordship after each demise or succession of any ruler. The life was further beset by the assumed right by attacking Islam to rule over larger and larger tracts in Bengal refusing to believe that the people could genuinely be interested in peaceful pursuit of happiness through development. The initial victory at Delhi gave them a further taste of riches that could be had by just not succumbing to the higher impulses of respect of human rights and fair-play for the people. The concepts of nationalism and strength in political unity for all Indians had not yet crystallised. The present day Jehadists of Pakistan are still labouring under the belief that India has not come out of the ancient days of disunity of rulers. They seem to believe that only there is camouflage of the basic disunity of various states of India which is often surfacing in sundry disputes and local rebellions of budding dictatorship of the right or the left.

3.2 Ilyas Shah and Spread of Islam

In 1335 A.D. governors appointed by the Sultan at Delhi ruled over three states in Bengal with capital cities at Satgaon, Sonargram and Lakhnauti. A soldier of fortune seized the capital city of Sonargram setting up a new Ilyas Shahi dynasty. Ilyas Shah declared his independence in 1337. Ibn Batuta visited Bengal in 1346. Feroz Shah Tughlak, the Sultan at Delhi sent an army to crush Ilyas Shah but did not succeed in so doing. During the reign of Ilyas Shah, Sylhet was conquered by an army led by a Muslim Darvesh Jalal Shah, i.e. a Muslim saint-soldier. Sylhet of Assam slowly became a Muslim majority area and during the partition of India, it was made a part of East Pakistan or of later day Bangladesh. The people of Sylhet welcomed the change of regime since the Hindu ruler was rather disliked because of his cruelty to his subjects.

The society was rigorously caste ridden and the yoke of priest craft was pitiless. The conversion to Islam offered an opportunity to quickly overcome caste oppression wherever the upper caste Hindus had not converted to Islam, since otherwise the caste prejudices were also carried over into Islam. A recent example of such continuation of prejudice is in the ethnically cleansed Pakistan Punjab. After independence a number of scheduled caste Hindus and 'untouchable' Hindu outcastes stayed on in West Pakistan claiming to be Christians, but slowly they managed to return to India finding that the 'caste conscious' Muslim converts continued to treat them as out-castes and excepting allowing them to worship in Christian manner, kept their social distance. (Now even Christian worship is precarious there.) The conversion to Islam was facilitated by incentive of official patronage often in the form of administrative or military employment. The courts appreciated conversion of accused persons and often gave them light punishment or many times a social position if the accused had some talent or money. On the other hand, if a convert became disillusioned, the Hindu society would not allow him to return to Hindu fold. This right to return has been rarely granted to Hindus. The only exception was in the case of Sindhis after the Arab conquest and violent rebellion against Arab rule there, or during and after the British rule by the Arya Samaj which is now active particularly in Hyderabad and South India with its headquarters in the Punjab. The right to reconvert was denied to Kashmiri neo-Muslims in the days of Akbar. Hindus rightly held that for spiritual growth all religions were equally valid and everyone should make efforts to perform good deeds in whichever faith he happens to operate. The popular mind solved the tangle in Bengal by identifying Siva with Adam and goddess Chandi with Eve. The gradual ascendancy of Tantra and magic was also the undoing of the gains that had accrued to Hinduism and Buddhism from logic, reasoning and acceptance of popular faiths and pilgrimages. Sahas Bodhaya in proto-Bengali script of 15th century has stories of magic and miracles glorifying Muslim fakirs and darveshes and tombs of Muslim fakirs and pirs. A host of Muslim saints and debaters and preachers descended on the areas of mixed population. They came from beyond India in the north-west and from Arabia and Iran in the wake of Ghazis and traders. Many *takyas* or centres of Muslim education and gurudom came into existence. Some are still active and flourishing with undercurrents of Pakistani obsessions. The pull of the Muslim Pir or guru was always as strong as that of the Hindu Rishi or guru. As late as forty years ago a Hindu family of Chandigarh moved to Karachi to be near their Pir who had gone to Pakistan leaving his Hindu faithful stranded in India! Islam could recognise many local men, ideas or objects as pirs for worship in that locality.

Islam was the religion then of patronage, one is surprised that more Hindus particularly lower castes and tribals including worshippers of Hindu or Buddhist pantheons did not succumb to conversion. These classes freely converted when convinced by the honesty and fellow feeling of the traders from the trading towns of Arabia and Iran or the preachers from Maldives or Arakan. It was, thus, that great majority of Hindus of present Bangladesh converted to Islam and unfortunately they too have been misled into Pakistani obsession of double standard of dealing: one for Muslims and another for non-Muslims according to their misinterpretation of the Koran. Anarchy and village autonomy worked against conversion. Distant authority was content if its tax collection was continuing. They found it more convenient to farm out tax collection to local chiefs whether Hindu or Muslim who were otherwise independent to guard, or to oppress the subjects. Widespread oppression led to political revolts but not religious revolts. Kings Husain Shah (1493–1519) and his son Nusrat Shah (1519–1552) were benevolent rulers and extended their protection to all subjects. Bengal was turning Vaishnava and the Vaishnavas adored Husain Shah regarding him as an Avatara of Krishna. Same kind of love was given by the Hindus to the Nawab Wajid Ali Shah of Awadh in the 19th century when the British

Company despoiled him of his wealth and power. King Husain Shah also received support from the Court of the assassinated rulers of Gauda. Soon Tripura and Orissa were also annexed. Husain Shah's times first saw the great outpouring of Bengali literature. Bipradas wrote Manasasch-Mangala in 1480 and he was the recipient of the first high Muslim honour of Gunraj Khan. In 1410 A.D. Ilyas Shah over-ran Dinajpur ruled by Ghias-ud-din Ahmed, the Dinajpur throne was usurped through court intrigue by one Raja Ganesh who set up his own Hindu dynasty which lasted a brief period of about thirty years. He honoured a Pandit Brihaspat with the title of Raj Mukut. His third successor was defeated by the Muslim ruler of Gaud.

During the Pala and Sena rules Sanskrit was the literary language. The 15th century could boast of Bengali songs of Vidyapati who was the court poet of raja Siva Sena. Vaishnava composers Chandidas, Krittivas and Parameshwar Das won great popularity. Sukar Mohammed's tale of Gopi Chand and queen Mainamati became popular. Earlier literature can be assessed from songs in Charyapada honouring Tantra. Mansa Mangal was composed in 1495. Jaideva Nanda wrote padavali lyrics, Kashiram Das and others wrote Mahabharata in Bengali which became favourite of both Hindus and Muslims of Bengal. Literature in Bengali language was also enriched by poets of Tripura who excelled in writing Puranic stories. Markandeya Puran was composed in 1530 by the court poet of Cooch Behar. Story of Nala Damyanti also originated there. Shashthi Mangal eulogises the Buddhist goddess Hariti who looks after the welfare of children. Syed Murtaza was the chief composer of padavalis honouring Radha and Krishna. Worship of Satyanarain was continued by neo-Muslims as of Satya pir and of Ban-Durga as Banbibi. Arakan composers gave Padmavati ballad. Shri Chaitanya (1485–1534) allowed women to participate in Kirtans and this became a regular Bengali event. New centres of Vaishnavism developed in Navadweep. Pilgrimage of Mathura-Vrindavan became common. The cultural activity continued irrespective of the court intrigues or Afghan-Mughal exertions against each other in numerous Hindu and Muslim capital cities. Raja Man Singh and his sons secured Bengal for Delhi emperors. Slowly a pattern of anarchy ensued which was of use to the European powers who successfully fished in troubled waters, enriching them as well as native merchants and collaborators.

Ilyas Shah had Pir Sirajuddin and Sheikh Biyabani visit Bengal. The Ilyas Shahi dynasty produced great builders. Many mosques, minarets and hammams were built from the material of the desecrated Hindu, Buddhist or Jain places of worship or Viharas for monks, etc. This is what defies analysis of Bengal archaeology from its ruins. Sultan Ilyas Shah exchanged an embassy with China. Bengal, according to a Chinese traveller, had a number of walled cities which participated fully in foreign trade which was the source of inflow of riches besides exporting the produce of Bengal mines and surplus of salt. People liked sport events like wrestling and pitting of one animal against another. The mid-day meals were often followed by song and dance. Pir Shah Jamal was responsible for the conquest of Sylhet in 1484. A grandson of Sultan Ibrahim of Gaur gifted a village (Chandpur) to Brahmans and had a Brahman as his minister. King Husain Shah had an unusual devotion to Bengali literature. He also chastised the Abyssenian usurpers and marauders of Gaur, killing about 12,000 of them. Such marauding mobs have often appeared in Indian history when the rule of law is lax. These kings believed in Bengal nationalism and gave full recognition to merit where they found it. Due to his zeal in upkeep and digging of new wells and tanks he was loved by the subjects. He settled many sufi pirs in Burdwan. A Buddhist relic continued to be revered, the Muslims calling it stone of Allah. He got a large mosque built in Chittagong.

Upto the 16th century, spreading of Islam in Bengal was only on the same lines as in the rest of north India. Concentration of Muslims in East Bengal occurred due to change in economic policy under the Moghuls. While greater control over anarchy was exercised by the central government, migration and settlement of Muslim peasants received encouragement by the introduction of wet cultivation of rice by immigrant Muslim peasants from other parts of Bengal and North India particularly eastern U.P. and Bihar. The peasants of East Bengal were more prosperous like the Sikh peasants settled in West Punjab on the canal irrigated land by the British in the early 20th century. On the partition of India the rice basket area fell in Pakistan while the Sikh peasantry of West Punjab had to escape with their lives to rest of India. The people of East Bengal still are often rioting against the minority Hindus.

3.3 Afghans and Mughals

Before the attack of Babar on the Lodhi emperors of Delhi after defeating the Rajput army of Rana Sanga, the Afghans had subdued most of the states of Hindu and Buddhist kings of Bengal. All over India the political power had been usurped by petty despots who governed with the willing or forced consent of feudal lords. Where the ruler was a protector of the subjects and had in addition the support of the Brahmans or the monks and ascetic orders and was charitable supporter of public works, temples or monasteries, and ruled with the object of contentment of the subjects, he approached the Hindu ideal of a ruler and his position was secure against unrest or rebellion of his subjects. His only undoing would be military defeat at the hands of another king. The political philosophy of the day permitted aggressive expansion and the ambition to become an over-lord or maharaja or emperor. Usually acknowledgement of subordination was all that was necessary along with the promise of some annual tribute. Thus inter-state anarchy was endemic to India from the days of the Hindu expansion of pre-historic period. There was a recognised period of the year when the armies of kings made their moves and counter-moves. The general public recognised this duty of their king and overlooked the inconvenience caused to themselves. The rules of the game were altered when the foreigners attacked Indian states, like the Huns, Sakas, or Kushans and particularly the tribal Muslims from West Asia. Earlier there was physical colonization and settlement of the foreigners in the capital cities or feudal forts, but they converted to Hindu practices and devotion to the common gods without particular displacement of Brahmans and Indian control of their temples and holy places. The Muslim conquest was different. They were not satisfied with mere acknowledgement of defeat and subordination. Later they would accept this sort of arrangement and make it their own way of feudal control, but for start they beheaded the local kings, decimated all military leadership or got them converted to their religion and give up worship of Hindu gods and idols. The Muslim conquest was of destructive nature and never had respite for widespread reconstruction in the interest of their subjects, majority of whom resisted conversion to Islam. The Hindus gave a performance which was morally impressive and often admired by thinking Muslims. The Rajput bravery and chivalry was unsurpassed except that they were not used to wage a war of winning tactics and foresight or advance planning involving Chanakya Niti. They persistently lost to the superior will and resolve and the waging of war by all means, fair or foul by the new aggressors. The uncertain security in the country from times immemorial had led to the climate of bribery and corruption. The stories and literature about the public and the gods from old times confirm this. After consolidation of their hold on Delhi and neighbourhood, the Muslim armies overran fort after fort of north India and were hammering at the borders of powerful kingdoms still present in the rest of India including the Gauda and the Orissa kingdoms in the east. Khilji raid in Bengal opened the way for centuries of aggression from Delhi emperors against Magadha, Bengal and Orissa kings. They had relatively more success in Bengal and the opposition was more fierce by the states to the east and north of Bengal. Assam and Orissa stayed practically independent upto the 16th century. Lodhi emperors, following the practice of the earlier Delhi Sultans, appointed governors over the conquered territories in Bengal. These governors now carried on the old policy of native kings in Bengal of military expansion of their territory. Because of turmoil and kingly anarchy, the governors indulged in the status of independent kingship sometimes paying lip service of loyalty to the Delhi emperor and sometimes murdering his appointees. Bengal of pre-Mughal period had many states ruled by independent Hindu or Afghan chiefs. Raja Ganesh (1410–1442) and the brief Hindu dynasty could not be any Hindu revival but only to be dismissed as a successful court intrigue and nothing more. Hemu would repeat this at the time of Mughal attack on Delhi.

The independent king Husain Shah had already succumbed to the expectation of his subjects, by becoming a just ruler. He has been hailed as an Akbar of Bengal. He entered on a truce with Babar in 1529. He had the golden mosque built in Gaur. Sufi pirs had settled in large numbers in Burdwan district. A splendid mosque was constructed in Chittagaon. Many mosques and dargahs were established in Dacca. The Baba mosque was built on the ruins of a temple. Jaffar Khan conquered Saptagaon. The Muslim divines and preachers worsted the monks in public debates. Hindu writers and poets wrote their Puranic stories and plays unmolested. They enriched budding Bengali literature by translating *Ramayana* and

Mahabharata. Sher Shah adopted the scorched earth policy in Gaur to avoid its capture by Humayun, but Humayun had to flee after his defeat by Afghans in Bihar in 1539 A.D. The Afghans, however, retained control in Dacca. Sher Shah created many feudatories. Mughals conquered Gaur only in 1576 A.D. and Sylhet in 1612. Akbar's general Man Singh conquered Orissa from an Afghan governor in 1592 A.D. Under Mughal peace after the capture of the strongholds of the Portuguese pirates in Chittagaon, the Bengal commerce picked up. Man Singh's capital was Akbar Nagar in Raj Mahal. Akbar's government and revenue collection system started functioning in Bengal in 1610 A.D. Bengal's exports of silk, fine cottons, indigo and textile goods as well as potteries and precious stones enriched the country. The European traders made all their purchases for export, in silver and gold. The European missionaries were unwittingly responsible for the renaissance in Bengal. Feminine literacy progressed due also to the Vaishnava movement. Naga gosains, darveshes and auliyas spread the Sufi philosophy of a loving God which was closer to Hinduism. The Sunnis, however, took pride in their fanatic Islamic faith and named Bengal as hell well stocked with food. With the mellowing down of the Kazis and Islamic courts, the Hindu administrators and revenue officials who were in large scale employment throughout the land helped in promotion of peace and economic progress as well as satisfactory income of various Afghan and Mughal courts. Raja Satrajit extended Mughal control in Cooch Behar and Assam. Later day Mughals were incompetent, there was a spate of rebellions and collection of revenue became more cruel irrespective of the ability of the peasants to pay up. The cities stayed prosperous. The dignitaries appointed by one ruler were dismissed by the successor. The anarchy could be controlled after the trading companies had found ways to further impoverish the land as well as demonstrate better administrative and military presence. The trading companies held the purse strings for the incompetent and idle warlords: Mughal or Afghan who indulged in irresponsible tax farming and direct tax collection.

3.4 Growth of Bengali Language

Bengali language, distinct from Sanskrit and the early *apbhransh* common to a large area including Bengal became the distinguishing element of the Bengalis during the Afghan and Mughal period. This gave a joint identity to the Hindus and Muslims of Bengal. A common Bengal culture could now be established and it was very much done. People began to identify Siva with Akbar, Kartik with Qazi, goddess Chandi with Eve (Amma Hava). Skandbodh written in Sanskrit (Bengali alphabet) has stories glorifying Muslim fakirs. King Hussain Shah, a patron of learning was popular with the Vaishnavas who regarded him as an incarnation of Krishna. Vipradas was awarded the title of Ganraj Khan. He wrote Mansasch Mangalam, (1480) which includes tales from the Puranas. Vidyapati wrote his poetry in Bengali in the 15th century. Many Vaishnava writers flourished in this century in Raja Siva Sena's court. The Buddhist treatise *Shunya Puran* was compiled. The Ramayana and the Mahabharata were translated into Bengali. Jaideva Nanda wrote Padavali lyrics. The Mahabharata written in Bengali by Kashi Nanda and his colleagues became the Bengali national classic loved both by Hindus and Muslims of Bengal. Sukar Muhammed's tale of Gopichand and his queen Mainamati was composed.

Rajmata of Tripura wrote Puranic stories. Biswas Sinha, the founder of the ruling dynasty of Kooch Behar had a court poet writing Bengali verse. Markandeya Puran was completed in 1530 and the tale of Nala and Damyanti in 1546. Folk literature appeared in the form of tales of Chand Saudagar. The worship of Satyanarayna or Satya Pir took root and the practice still flourishes especially with the Bengalis outside Bengal. Bauls and Muslim darveshes spread the cultivation of Ali Raja. Glorification of Muslim saints and heroes was composed in Bengali, e.g. Shah Muhammed's Sulekha and Yusuf. He also wrote life of Muhammed or Nabi Vansh. Syed Murtaza was the composer of padavali about the love of Radha and Krishna. There was a shower of Bengali literature from the followers of Shri Chaitanya. From mid 15th to mid 18th centuries. Renaissance in Bengal literature occurred during the company rule with the advent of European scholars.

3.5 An Epilogue

Stewart in his history of Bengal lists twenty independent kings from 1340 to 1530 A.D. They usually ascend the throne under the adage "might is right". There is a continuous story of aggression and rebellion. The kings were in continuous strife with rebels and possible successors or neighbours. They often oppressed Hindu subjects particularly if they tried to conceal wealth from the taxman. The kazis were lenient if the guilty accepted conversion to Islam. In the kingly adventures, while the Indian rules prescribed fair treatment and usually confirmation of the opponent when he accepted subordination, the Muslim rules of war were more harsh usually demanding total subjugation or placing hostages with the victor. The military campaigns and victories however did not over much disturb the even tenor of rural life. Hindus continued to live and prosper in the Muslim capital or cantonment cities. The Hindu rulers of Assam, and Orissa withstood most attacks and sometimes won victories and imposed their own terms. Hindus and Muslims however were developing friendly private and commercial relations.

After the independent kings, came the Sher Shah dynasty and Delhi appointed governors (thirty-one in number from 1576 to 1756). The usual in-fighting continued. But the state was also busy in improving road and river communications. Sher Shah Suri's famous policy about maintenance of roads and better facilities for road users continued. Sikander Shah (1358–1393) was a great builder of mosques and minarets and the ruins are a puzzle to archaeologists since they include pell-mell the artefacts from earlier Hindu and other non-Muslim structures. There seemed now a sense in including many gods and goddesses in people's prayers. A common Bengal culture was evident. Liquor and *bhang* were sold in public and did not draw any kazi's ire. Cowrie was the common man's currency which lingered upto 1850.

Sher Shah had seized Gaur in 1538 and made Bengal safe for Afghans. The Mughals conquered Gaur in 1576 and Sylhet in 1612. Akbar conquered Orissa in 1592. Mughal viceroy in Bengal conquered Chittagong and the foreign trade picked up again. The rebels in East Bengal and in the deltaic region were soon after swept away. The mixing of Bengali people for evolving a Bengali nation occurred in Mughal period, the build-up having begun since the arrival of Sufis in hordes since they were being expelled from Delhi by the tyrannical Muslim ulema.

4

Failure of Autocracy

Long ago after experimenting with oligarchy, theocracy, priestly rule and democracy, the Indian public found the most workable proposition in benevolent monarchy or an autocracy acceptable to the influential classes and following the scriptural qualities of kingship. The public continued to have the right to rebel and be governed by a new kingly personality. Their undoing was on two accounts. In order to assure security of their small states, they assumed the right to expand their territory and power leading to perpetual conflict of various states and convulsive search for large empires. Such empires in those days of limited communications soon broke up particularly when foreign invaders took a hand, who were strangers to the gentlemanly struggle of Indian states for supremacy. The foreign victors took advantage of Indian proneness to kingly discipline, but developed unalloyed autocracy. They did not accept correction by their own civil and military advisers and accepted no authority over themselves. The second major failure of all autocracy has been every king's goal of having his son as his successor irrespective of the son's faults and unsuitability for the high office. The highest bureaucratic authority had no training schools or teachers to learn the art of kingly actions. Wherever this became possible, the succession became normal but usually it was the occasion of civil war and turmoil.

The Delhi Sultans and the great Mughals were autocrats, veritable Napoleons in their courts without modern technology which can project central authority even at distant corners of the realm. The governors and administrators appointed by them soon discovered that they wholly depended on the goodwill of the king and their position suffered from all kinds of court intrigue and conspiracies and further if they declared themselves as independent kings, they could easily get away with a huge prize. An autocrat was always a target of an assassin especially if the assassin had the goodwill of some of the king's lords of the army or the high priests etc. The king had the resources to reward loyalty at the cost of the public so long as the king's own coffers bulged with wealth. King's major resource of wealth were revenue and taxes on trade. If the king could not tread the virtue of benevolence, no one could coerce him to be just and fair. Autocratic rule was sore beset with wars of succession, rebellions and assassinations. The whole history of Afghan and Mughal rule is studded with such disasters. To add to the woes of autocrats, most of the Bengal rulers identified themselves with the Muslim faction of the public but had to satisfy not the neo Muslims but the immigrant Muslims from west Asia who regarded themselves as the pillars of the Sultanate and the Mughal rule but for the earned share in the imperial glory of the Rajputs and some talented Hindu individuals. In Bengal, the administration stayed in the hands of the petty Hindu officials particularly because of the autonomy exercised by the villages. Democracy had a chance to take root only with the advance in trading and capital financing of industry and farming.

In line with the normal kingly duties, all governors and kings in Bengal constantly tried to expand their power by strife with their neighbours. The struggles of Afghan and Mughal factions at Delhi cast a big shadow in Bengal. Afghans took couple of centuries to snatch power from Hindu rulers and another two centuries were spent in Mughal-Afghan struggle. But before Mughals could carry on any reconstruction they were to contend with superior ability and resources and new morality of the Europeans and the new upsurge in culture and wealth of the Hindus who opted for modern education and collaboration with European trading companies. Their disillusionment with the British and successful fight for Indian freedom is quite another story.

Ibrahim Khan, son of Ali Mardan governor appointee by Shah Jehan was fair-minded and punished oppressors among the tax-collectors. On the other hand, Shobha Singh of Midnapore appointed by the Afghan Rahim Khan of Orissa, plundered Murshidabad, the capital city of the Delhi Sultans in Bengal. He also forced Kasimabad to pay ransom. As a consequence of such lawlessness, the Europeans could proceed to fortify their settlements. The subedar Murshid Quli

Khan founded an independent dynasty. Same was done by governor Ali Vardi Khan. There were wide-spread political conspiracies and administrative corruption. New land based aristocracy (confirmed later by Lord Cornwalis in English Company dominated areas) further impoverished the peasants and ordinary citizens while the aristocracy with no productive functions flourished dipping into the public revenues and tax collections on internal and external trade. This led to many famines and further misery prevailed on account of raids by the Marathas who polished the system of collection of ransom money or enforced revenue collection rights (first farmed out by the Delhi rulers and then snatched by European companies). These were now the aimed spoils of Maratha incursions and threats.

Shuja-ud-din who succeeded Murshid Ali Khan, was acknowledged by the Delhi emperor as Shuja-ud-Daula. He had managed to send tribute to Delhi and so was acknowledged by them as the ruler of Bengal. From then on the myth of Delhi being the over-lord of whole of India who could be coerced to grant kingship of any territory of India on the promise of some annual tribute, took root. All kings needed money and only recourse was squeezing of the subjects directly or indirectly. All oppression however by local rulers or tribute promising European companies was carried out in the name of the emperor at Delhi. Shuja-ud-Daula had scrupulous regard for justice, but in his old age he was partial to luxury and profligacy.

Mir Habib, a Murshidabad general conquered Tippererah while political corruption scuttled the prosperity of Murshidabad and of Dacca. Still they were quite strong militarily and could discipline Birbhum when it revolted and they helped Orissa get back the idol of Shri Jagannath for Puri so that the pilgrim route in the control of Bengal and Orissa could continue to enrich them. They however could not prevent the entrenched European powers in Bengal from blocking the entry of the Germans in the lucrative Bengal trade. In 1744, Ali Vardi threatened the gem traders of Europe thus decimating the Dutch income as well as his own. The traders started to carry out private trade under bogus tax exemption labels. This further reduced the gains of foreign companies as well as reduced the tax collection. Shuja-ud-Daula imposed many new taxes and levies. To meet Maratha demands, Ali Vardi pressured the foreign companies. When the

Marathas occupied Orissa in 1755, there was a big blow to Bengal as powerful Afghan claimants attacked Mughal authorities in Bengal. Organized loot of Bengal started in 1751 by the Sanyasis and fakirs, mostly rebellious soldiers from various factions now united as marauders and adopting holy garb. Soon Lord Clive of the English East India Company took a hand as master conspirator in removing the honest king and placing his nominees on the Bengal throne for getting coveted revenue and administrative rights from him for exploiting both, the Bengal rulers and the ruled.

4.1 Co-existence of Ordinary People in the 18th Century Bengal

Co-existence of various castes and creeds existed keeping the requisite social distance. People were divided by caste, religion and region. The social distance between the upper and lower classes was there though they mixed in religious processions and pilgrimages. There was respect for the assumed higher status of upper classes and higher castes. A higher status Muslim could not allow proximity to a Muslim of lower status. This was the Hindu style of co-existence and stability in stratified society. The people were quite absorbed in family matters. There was assumed grading among Muslims based on assumed closeness to Shariat teaching. Pecking order was diligently maintained both among the Hindus as well as the Muslims. The craftsmen served higher castes living separately from them. There were restrictions on partaking of food and in marriage. Marriage was arranged entirely by the family. Excommunication and community fines were common. Only the Sikhs held *langars* where all were welcome and invited to eat sitting together. Services rendered by craftsmen like barbers, weavers, embroiderers, dyers, gardeners, and potters were recompensed in the traditional manner at harvest time or on the occasion of family celebrations.

Female infanticide was common. Since honour of un-married girls was always in danger, custom of early marriage of girls prevailed and was recommended in scriptures. The seclusion of women was wide-spread and had spread to non-Muslims as well. Women on the whole were not educated. Rural population had no schools worth the name. Sati was common in Bengal. Polygamy was a sign of family prosperity and prevailed in Bengal. Widow re-marriage was not permitted. (The Peshwa had imposed a tax on widow re-marriage in the Maratha domains.) The lot of Hindu widows was pitiable. There was sale in India of Hindu or Muslim slaves. Foreign born slaves were treated as cheap servants. Feudal system of hereditary retainers existed. Senior-most wife had precedence, but the children of all wives had equal rights. Divorce was usually avoided even among Muslims, while it was not allowed by Hindu religion. There was no intermarriage between orthodox Shia and Sunni families. Seclusion of sexes before marriage was practised. Only politically entrenched families could think of inter-religious marriages. Education and training was restricted to what was essential for entering the family profession. Children were treated as apprentices with no organized institutions of learning. Only high caste Hindus could billet their children on the Guru's household for learning. Teachers belonged to Brahman or Kayastha castes. Kathas and Kirtans were popular source of instruction. Muslim masses were steeped in ignorance except in what they gathered from religious processions and Mahabharata etc. popular dance dramas or as retainers for future army service. Most of high society literature or poetic efforts, were in Urdu language which was not commonly understood in Bengal. The poetry was full of obsolete references and dying metaphors. Certain feudal chiefs gave patronage to writers and poets. The Hindus routinely prayed for more wisdom while the Muslims awaited Allah's kind attention. The Muslims of the 18th century Bengal had neither the wish nor the capacity to follow Shariat. The new doctrine of Wahdat Ul Wajud was indifferent to moral laxity. It was allowing some kind of acceptance of non-Muslim philosophy and created distrust of Shariat. Shah Wali-Ullah translated the Koran into Persian to make it more accessible to Indians who preferred to learn Persian than Arabic. Sheikh Ahmed of Sarhind claimed that the new doctrine was undermining the Shariat. Jan-I-Janan was murdered by a Shia since he had poured ridicule over regarding of tazias as sacred by Shias. The Muslims and Hindus were joining in the worship of Khwaja Khizr and Goga pir, reminders of the ancient snake worship. Strangely, the Bishnois prayer of namaz continued when facing east as they did while praying as Hindus. Caste drove the Husaini Brahmans to accept charity only from the Muslims since they regarded Muslims, being their former patrons and later converted to Islam, as of the right caste. Some Muslim groups followed both Hindu and Muslim customs. They would dance before Kali and participate as pilgrims in prayers before temple idols in Vrindaban which continued to attract them as a religious magnet. Belief in the efficacy of charms and fasts was wide-spread. Holi was a common seasonal festival for both Hindus and Muslims. Lack of law and order was a curse affecting all the public: Hindus or Muslim. The cities stood plundered. The industry and trade languished while waiting for the advent of Europeans on the scene which would be a mixed blessing.

5

New Upsurge of Bhakti

People turn to prayer and devotional love of God in the times of unrest and insecurity. The Punjabis had their Sikh Gurus and Sufi saints, the Marathas will have later their saint poets and witnessed myriads of faith inspiring miracles. In Bengal devotional songs and prayers of Vaishnava poets burst forth meaning a new leaf in the book of Hinduism. While Ram Katha Kirtans were providing solace to Hindus of the heartland of India, Radha Krishna Sankirtans gave a new cultural awakening to the Bengalis: rich or poor, Hindu or Muslim. Later it would be the cult of mother Kali. In the 10th century, Jaideva was busy in Lakshman Sena's court writing *Gita Govinda*. The *Gita Govinda* is a classic of Sanskrit literature and influenced a great deal the religious thinking especially in Bengal. (Sena kings controlled territory upto Mithila and Nepal and Narasimha, the king of Jajnaga had expelled the Islamic control in Radhe or southern Bengal.) Vidyapati (1370–1460) wrote Padavali in Sanskrit. He composed many Bengali songs and was the court poet of Raja Shiv Sena. Other eminent poets included Chandidas (1417–1477), Sri Krishna Kirti and some Vaishnava poets and composers. Shri Chaitanya (1486–1534) has been hailed as an Avatara of Krishna. He was an indefatigable preacher of Vaishnavism and Bhakti of Krishna. His times also were of comparative stability and peace in Bengal. Kings Husain Shah and Nusrat Shah patronized Bengali literature. Vipradas wrote Mansa-chaMangal in 1480 and was awarded the highest literary title of Gunraj Khan. It was the first award to a Hindu poet in Muslim rule of Bengal. Women were welcome to participate in Chaitanya's Vaishnava Kirtans and processions. Nityanand Prabhu, Advait acharya, Gadadhar Pandit and Srivas Thakur were some other associates of Chaitanya Mahaprabhu who spread his message far and wide. The Rajput influence in Mughal rule was a great help in the spread of Vaishnavism. Puri became more favoured pilgrim centre. Lord Chaitanya travelled to Puri and on the way rested at Dantan, a road junction which gained popularity on that account. Many ancient temple ruins in this area show vestiges of Siva and Jain worship. Other great Vaishnava teachers in Panchkot area were Mahaprabhu Shivaram Goswami and Trilochan Goswami. The Jains freely accepted Vaishnavism since the accent on vegetarianism and non-violence and love of fellow beings is similar in the two faiths. Even primitive Mundas, Tamar and Bundu tribals of Ranchi district became Vaishnava singing Vaishnava songs in their dialects. Many Jain statues in ancient temples are still worshipped as Hindu deities, apparently because of error, but in reality because in Bengal Hinduism had always been inclusive of Buddhism and Jainism and was slowly and surely engulfing Indian Islam till recent times when imperial politics took a hand in obstructing the growing unity among Indians which reached its full stature with Subhas Chandra Bose.

Literature in the Bengali language was also enriched by the poets of Tripura who excelled in propagating Pauranic stories. Markandeya Puran was composed in 1530 by the court poet of Cooch Behar. Shashthi Mangal eulogises the Buddhist goddess Hariti who looks after the welfare of children. Sayyed Murtaza was the chief composer of Padavalis honouring Radha and Krishna. Worship of Satyanarayana was continued by neo-Muslims as of Satya Pir. Pilgrimage to Mathura-Vrindavan became very common. The cultural activity continued despite court intrigues. Bhakti was enriched by the crop of great poets like Jaideva, Chandidas. Vidyapati and Chaitanya. Rajput presence in Bengal helped the growth of Krishna cult and so did the pilgrim centre of Puri. The Jains became Krishna Bhakts *enmasse*. Even Mundas became Vaishnava followers. There exist old Munda songs about love of Radha and Krishna. The Vaishnavas frequently visit Jain temples. In Bengal Hinduism had become fully inclusive of Buddhism and Jainism. The growing unity among all Indians reached its peak under the leadership of Netaji in the INA.

The European missionaries were unwittingly responsible for the renaissance in Bengal. Feminine literacy progressed due to the

Vaishnava movement. Naga gosains, Muslim darveshes and auliyas spread the sufi philosophy of loving God, thus bringing Muslims closer to Hindus and slowly Bengal became more integrated than any other part of India. The Sunni Muslims however were wedded to their worship of uncompromising Islamic claims of exclusive closeness to God. With the mellowing down of the Kazis and Islamic courts, the Hindu administrators and revenue officials employed in large numbers throughout the land became the new aristocracy. Landlords and traders worked for peace and creation of wealth for the upkeep of parasitic courts. The anarchy would end only after further impoverishment of the peasantry and the cruelty of irresponsible revenue collection.

5.1 Jaideva, Vidyapati, Chandidas and Chaitanya

People turn to Bhakti more at the times of crisis in their lives and also when there is too much philosophical argumentation. Muslim invasions of Bengal started in 1202 A.D. Thirteenth century was also the century of Jaideva in king Lakshman Sena's court. The Sena rule extended to Mithila and Nepal. Centre of Islamic learning was established at Lakshmanvati after the defeat of Jajnaga (Raja Narasimha) who had earlier annihilated Muslim invasion forces of Radhe. There was no open oppression of Hindus even in Muslim strongholds. Hindu rule was continuing in Assam, east Bengal, and Orissa. Jaideva's *Gita Govinda* is a classic of Sanskrit literature it exerted great influence on religion and philosophy of Bengal.

Vidyapati (1370-1460) wrote *Padavali* in Sanskrit. His songs were in Bengali language and he was the poet laureate of king Shiv Sena. Chandidas (1417-1477) wrote *Sri Krishna Kirti*. He led a group of Vaishnava poets in Shiv Sena court that included Parmeswara Das. Shri Chaitanya Mahaprabhu was the spirit behind the Krishna Bhakti of that period. Chaitanya lived during the period of relative peace and security provided by the secularist rule of Hussain Shah (1493-1519) and Nusrat Shah (1519-1552) who patronized the great age of Bengali literature. We have already mentioned how Vipra Das wrote *Mansasch Mangal* (1480) and was awarded the title of Gunraj Khan. Women were allowed to participate in Chaitanya's Kirtans which led to education and uplift of Bengal women. Nityanand

Prabhu, Advaita Acharya, Gadadhar Pandit, Srivas Thakur were some of the exalted associates who spread the message of Chaitanya far and wide in Bengal and Orissa. In recent times, an ardent devotee, Bhakti Vedant Mahaprabhu, regarded as an incarnation of Chaitanya has by his devotion and his rendering of Harinam Kirtans spread a new Krishna Consciousness movement all over the world with centres established in India as well as in many other countries. Sahajiya and Ahajiya cults of post Chaitanya period spread the doctrine of self-realization through love of wife or some other woman. Many devotional sects are flourishing even now : Aul, Baul, Sai, Darbara and Kirtbhaja. The devotees are both Hindu or Muslim.

Lord Chaitanya travelled to Puri and on the way rested at Danton which has become an important Vaishnava centre on that account. Sasanka, the seventh century king of Gaur had dug a large tank there which is still in use but now known as Sarsanka tank commemorating some local chieftain of the Ganga dynasty who probably had it renovated in the eleventh century. The powerful Rajput chief of Purulia who had established a Panchayat Raj there, converted to Vaishnavism. Practically the entire population became Vaishnava by the middle of the nineteenth century after having been Saivites or Jains in the past. Mahaprabhu Shivarama Goswami (a Vaishnava) had a large following in the Panjkot Raj. The Jains freely converted to Vaishnavism. Mundas became Vaishnava in Purulia and neighbouring Banda and Tamar areas of Ranchi district. There are old Munda songs about the love of Radha and Krishna. Bhumij community of Purulia also became Vaishnava. There are considerable number of ruined Jain temples in the region and sometimes, a Jain statue is in loving worship by the Hindus. The Vaishnavas have four divisions: Nimbark, Shree, Vishnu Swami, and Madhav. Ramanuji and Ramanandi sections both belong to the Shree category.

6

Evolution and Integration of Society

Large influx of Brahmans of north India and Muslim traders and immigrants entered Bengal from Arabia and Iran in the wake of trade. Bengal was the chief centre of trade with South East Asia. Many illuminated manuscripts of Pala days have been unearthed. There are Brahmanical subjects engraved in copper plates. The society believed in the co-existence of primitive castes and tribes like Kola, Saraba, Pulandas, Hadi, Dom, Chandal, and Nishads. Most Bengalis were deemed to be Kshatriyas with whom immigrant higher castes could inter-marry. *Brihad Puran* indicates the conditions from the Pala days. The Sudras were subdivided into thirty-six sub-castes. The Brahmans were allowed to eat meat and fish according to the Bengal Dharam Shastras. Brahmans could also become fighters or agriculturists. The marriageable age for girls was reduced to eight. The Devala Brahmans engaged in astrology or in painting had lower status.

Non-Brahman castes included Karna castes engaged in the profession of scribes. Barbers and potters as well as painters often belonged to Sudra castes. Nagar Brahmans traced their ancestory to imported Brahmans from the Punjab and Kamboj Brahmans from U.P. Bengal art and literature had distinct trait of aesthetics and optimism. Raja Kshitisena divided Radhiya Brahmans into grades depending on their extent of learning : Mukhya Kulins, Gaura Kulins, and Sadiya Kulins. According to Brihaspati Misra, king Vallal Sena graded Brahmans according to their learning, but soon the learning came to be included in inherited virtues at birth for the Siddha Shrotiya, Radheya Shrotiya or Kashtha Shrotiya Brahmans.

Muslim women were held in seclusion and *purdah* was spreading to Hindu women. Caste consciousness was seeping into Muslims.

Shia Sunni intermarriages were unimaginable. Women, especially Muslim women were steeped in ignorance. Masses were illiterate, but imbibed Indian culture from epics and religious discourses and Pauranic stories. Education was purely utilitarian and extremely narrow. Hindu influence was visible in the Islamic Wahid-ul-Wajud movement which was criticized by the orthodox Muslims of Sirhind. The Muslims did not follow the Shariat closely. The Bisnois said their namaz facing east the way the Hindus prayed. They uttered Vishnu and Bismallah together. Certain Muslims followed both Hindu and Muslim religious practices. The sect of Shivanarainis was popular with Muslims. A cult of Mian-Bibi was spreading with echoes of Hindu god-goddess pairs. Popularly held faith in amulets and charms brought Hindus, Muslims, lower castes, all in the same pail. Progress in civilization was stalled for all due to oppression and limited enterprise. Muslims who claimed to be descended from immigrants from Delhi, Kashmir, Iran, Iraq or Arabia regarded themselves as Ashraf (superior) to other Muslims and refused to interdine or intermarry with them. Islam too developed stratified stability like that of the Hindus.

6.1 Bengali Language and Beliefs

Yuan Tsang, the 7th century Chinese treveller noted love of learning among the populace of Bengal. Chandra Gosain in 500 A.D. founded the Chànder school of Sanskrit grammar. In the 7th and the 8th centuries the Bengal diction had noticeable departure from the classical style. The Bengal diction was called Gauda Riti. Bhatta Bhavdeva prepared a Vyavhar Tilaka, a manual of good manners, possibly under influence of Chinese Confucianism. A Bengali script had already evolved by the third century A.D. There was a distinct school of Bengal Dharam Sastra, the leading authority being Jemut Vahan. In the 12th century, a Radheya brahman expounded the Hindu law of succession. The spoken language was used in explaining the Hindu Dharma by the Vajrayna Siddhas in the 12th century. The Mahayana scholar, Shilbhadra became the pupil of Dharampala at Nalanda and he lectured far and wide on this theme. Teachers and preachers from Bengal took the Mahayana doctrines to Tibet where they were known as Atisa. The chief Atisa was Padmasambhava who was a colleague of Santirakshita, a teacher of Nalanda university. Padmasambhava silenced in debate the spokesmen of Bu Pa, the indigenous Tibetan faith.

In 1200 A.D. a poetry symposium had more than 500 entries. The medieval Vaishnavism inspired Jaideva and Saran, poets in king Lakshman Sena court to express in Sanskrit erotic devotional sentiments with pictorial richness and lyrical splendour. The mystic Charya poems belong to the 9th century dealing with mysticism of Sahaj-Yoga. The proto-Bengali language was visible from about 800 A.D. as Magadhi Prakrit and *Apbhransh*. Bengali art and culture was already being assimilated in Burma, Nepal, Tibet and other south east Asian countries. Bengal became the centre of the Tantric faith to which all Hindus (including Buddhists) converged. Bengal was the home of many Yogis who ranged far and wide making disciples. Guru Gorakhnath who established his seat in west Punjab was also one of them. The Yogis claimed all kinds of miraculous capabilities and the majority of Yogis at any time have been Bengalis. The yogic claims about miracles, however could not withstand the onslaught of reason and Islamic faith, as they had practically ignored the high level of ethics that goes with proper Yoga. Mysticism has a hold in Bengal. Saraha, Nagpodi, Tilpada and Nirapada of Varendra who were all disciples of Jetari wrote mystical poems in old Bengali. The Yoga discipline required training in Mantra, Mandals and Mudra that is incantations, intricate designs and hand and face gestures. The mystic aptitude was classified as Kula, Dambhi, Nati, Chandali or Brahmani. The whole system merged in Hinduism by the 14th century. The Bengal Hindus took to all kinds of beliefs in their stride forward including Sufism of Islam. Thus the gods came, flourished, were swept away either to oblivion or to museums and ruins. Still Siva and Shakti have proven long lasting besides the later Bhakti cults of Vaishnavism. Kartikeya or Surya almost lie forgotten in museums; popular Jainism is flourishing. Ruins of some large Jain temples are present at Paharpur. Jain Vihars of Digamber monks were in great profusion in the 7th century while the Buddhist Hinayana spread by Sri Lankan preachers was prominent in medieval Vanga. Buddhist monasteries at one time were spread all over Bengal before the 9th century and some still survive. Major survival is the worship of the Ganga and the worship of Siva. Along with Bengal

Vaishnavism, 16th century saw a vigorous popularity of Vaishnava lyrics. Sena period had earlier produced many popular lyrical ballads.

With the renaissance in the 19th century came a flood of poetry and literature in modern Bengali. Tagore, and Nazr-ul-Islam are quite recent. Bankim Chandra Chatterjee was the Indian Dickens and was followed by others.

There was a strong current of Islamic syncretistic tradition in Bengal. Ballads were composed regarding the imaginary exploits of pirs and fakirs. The blending of Islamic and Bengali traditions took place. There was a *fatwa* from the new reformers of Islam against popular Islam that included joint celebrations of traditional *poojas* and processions for rural and village deities including devotion to popular mythical pirs. The esoteric touch of Fakiri reflected the age-old reverence for monks of the Hindu faith that included Buddhist or Jain traditions. Sharp attacks from Wahabis and Hanafis disturbed the peasants in Bengal villages. A fatwa declared the Bengali language as the language of the Hindus and bewailed that the Bengali Muslims had become practicing Hindus. Popular Islam was accepting Nath Yogis and their beliefs. The mediators or the popular mood reconciled the mystical disciplines with the Sharia. Shaikh Chand wrote Hari-Gowrie Samvad glorifying the common version of creation of the universe upto the revelation of the Koran. Pada compositions of Alam had Vaishnava flavour. Shaikh Faiz Allah is credited with incorporation of Viashnavism and Nathism with Islam. Shri Chaitanya's philosophy of love was linked to Sufi inspiration. There were Muslim poets who wrote on the theme of Krishna and Radha. The Muslim poets developed the rural tradition of fictitious pirs and thus regularised many a local mode of worship, e.g. Mansa-pir, Satya pir, Khwaja Khizer, Pir Badar, Ghazi Pir (a son of Shiva and Parvati).

6.2 Indianness of Bengal with Sufi input

An essential ingredient in the integrated Indianness of Bengal is the contribution of Sufism. Sufis were a mystic offshoot of Islam that developed in West Asia which had the legacy of Manicheism, a syncretistic religion based on Hindu and Zoroastrian concepts along with those of Christianity. Mysticism was very much a part of these religions. The famous Sufi *silsilas* (houses) had contacts with Nath Yogis who combined Hindu and Buddhist Tantrism along with Yoga of Patanjali. The Sufis believed in the immanence of God and His direct accessibility for the pious Muslims and followers of Sufi discipline. Both Shias and Sunnis regarded Sufis as heretics. In the early centuries of Islam, some Sufis of Iran and Delhi were condemned to death by the Sunni dominated courts. Many leading Sufis from west, particularly their centres in Bukhara hopped over Multan and Delhi to spread in India with the sole purpose of Muslim expansion in India. Bengal became the main Sufi centre in India. In the beginning of the 19th century scores of Sufi centres (*Khanqas*) existed in Bengal. The Sufis adopted simple and frugal lives. They were liberal in giving charity and establishing communal *langars* for free meals. They subscribed to the belief that a preceptor was necessary for treading the spiritual path. Most bright young Muslims sought well known Sufi saints as preceptors. After a considerable period as initiates they were admitted to a chosen Sufi order. One could be a member of more than one *silsila* or order of Sufis. Sufis chose the path of asceticism and non-possession like that of Buddhist *bhikshus* or Hindu mendicants. The Sufis were loyal Shias or Sunnis if left to their own piety and began to be influenced by the piety in others. Guru Nanak and his disciples in the Punjab, Kabir at his loom in Varanasi and Vaishnavas of Bengal freely intermingled with the Sufis. Finding India congenial to their mode of worship. Sufis thronged into India from all corners of the world. They helped people to accept Islam by presenting a more familiar stance in Islam to the native population. From the beginning Muslims were advised also by the Sufis to be specially helpful to other Muslims. In Bengal the popular Vaishnavism required everyone to be helpful to others without exception. Sufis also began to welcome others to their samas (congregations involving prayer songs) and intermingled with Nath yogis and Vaishnavas. All the busy routes were dotted with *Khanqas* for the benefit of all travellers.

In India, famous Sufi saints had established *Khanqas* at Delhi and Agra which are still attracting both Hindu and Muslim pilgrims. The Sunnis regarded Bengal a rebel state since the hold of Sunnis there was not so strong. The social and cultural meeting place in Bengal was the Sufi *takyas* or *khanqas*. Hindus, Buddhists and Jains climbed down from exclusive hold on their gods to popular Saivite and Tantra philosophy. These philosophies gave way to trust once again in magic and yoga centred miracles of Nath yogis. The people began moving from yogic miracles to Muslim style miracles of Sufis. Most people did not offend miracle mongers whether Sufi or Nath and lent ear to both. The Hindu and Muslim peasants and rural population particularly lived comfortably together indulging in joint celebrations, entertainment and religious processions. The goal of Hindu and Sufi mysticism was identical and the paths similar. The identity of religious pursuits was further endorsed by practical confirmation by Sri Ramakrishna, a priest in a Kali temple of Calcutta.

Baba Farid was a famous Sufi poet of Punjab. Nizam-ud-din Aulia was a disciple of the Baba. He like the Hindu ascetics extolled renunciation to be the key to spiritualism. Penances, austerity, meditation and contemplation and conversation with other Sufis and yogis was routine for the Sufis. The Ilyas Shahi dynasty of Bengal rulers besides spreading Islam also provided a stimulus for the growth of a composite Bengal culture. Shaikh Haqq believed in Wahdut-ul-Wajud which excited an echo in Hindu philosophy. From the 15th century the Bengal Sufism was fused with indigenous mysticism. The Sharqi dynasty of Jaunpur saw to the establishment of Chishtiya and Suhravardi *silsilas*. The fusion was personified in the belief in Shah Madar the spiritual master of all entertainers Hindu or Muslim and in the evolution of Baul singing in both Hindu and Muslim sponsored gatherings. They had an esoteric vocabulary using Hindu-Buddhist words but having allegoric meaning in Islamic terms. Lal Ded, a Saivite poetess turned Sufi stormed Kashmiri Muslims. *Amrit Kunda* a Tantric treatise on yoga was translated into Persian. Many Muslims of Kashmir refuse to be known as Shias or Sunnis but wish only to be identified with the Rishi order of Sufis or Kashmiri Islam. Many Nath yogis popularized the syncretistic beliefs. To them Mohammed was a disciple of a yogi of Gujarat. The popularity of Vaishnava themes in Sufi sama gatherings was a remarkable development in the unity in diversity theme so popular in Hinduism. The Sikh gurus preferred worldly life to asceticism since that provided a harder test of piety.

6.3 British Ploy to combat Nationalism through Separate Electorates

The British decided to combat nationalism through separate electorates. There was a possibility that if democratic majority were to mean Hindu majority to the Muslims, they could be set up to oppose democratic freedom in India. The general feeling of Bengal Muslims in 1937 was of economic exploitation and domination by the better educated and more prosperous Hindus. The cohesion achieved in the 19th century was ebbing fast. The Muslim aristocracy in Bengal was almost all of foreign origin and had kept aloof from the Muslim peasants. For a long time the court language had been Persian and now most business was conducted either in English or in Bengali. The new Muslim reformers had obtained a fatwa that Bengali language was not to be encouraged by the Muslims. The nationalist Congress had broad support of the Muslim intellectuals but the Congress leaders failed to read the trend in the Muslim disquiet. Inadvertently in their pride of national awakening, they pushed the local Muslim leaders into the Muslim League fold. The Muslim league deplored the Quit India movement of the Congress and practically invited the British to stay on in India till Muslims had a satisfactory deal involving the Congress and the imperial British. The dream of some Bengal leaders of an independent Bengal with Bengali hegemony in east India was swept away by the landslide direct action of illiterate masses, both Muslim and Hindu, expressed in rioting and destruction of property. The famine of 1942 had already weakened the administration and everyone seemed to heave a sigh of relief when the British departed leaving British India in two parts, each thirsting for the destruction of the other but for the Congress leadership which continued to swear by secularism and India to be a secular state granting full human rights to all its citizens.

Slavery was a part of Muslim culture. They also had been mistakenly reading in their scriptures that all non-Muslims were kafirs and apostates with no rights. The top leaders of the league including Mr. Jinnah had agreed to the direct action of rioting and looting as a tactic only while they continued to profess Humanism, and minority rights in Pakistan. The minorities no longer trusted the league protestations and there were gigantic shifts of population. The partition of the Punjab and Bengal was particularly tragic for these states as well as for the whole subcontinent. The activation of SAARC over the lethargy of Pakistan only holds some promise for future peace and progress of both India and Pakistan. The split in Pakistan on the basis of language presages more cooperation between India and other countries of South Asia including Pakistan. Bengali would easily become the second international language of South Asia second only to English which is now become a language of preference in India and to some extent in Pakistan.

6.4 Arts and Crafts

The Bengal intellectuals have been in the fore-front of revival of arts and crafts. They excelled in writing sonnets. Girish Chander Ghosh was the founder of the national theatre. Dr. Mahendralal Sarkar founded the Bengal Science Association in 1867. The Indian Association for the Cultivation of Science was formed in 1870. Contributions of Sir J.C. Bose, and Acharya Prafulla Chander Roy are famous. Rabindranath Tagore was awarded the Nobel prize for literature, he was a multi-dimenstional genius: poet, philosopher, composer, essayist, novelist, critic, playwright, engaged in village reconstruction and the new education at the Vishwa Bharati set-up by him. Songs composed by him provide national anthems to India and Bangladesh. The Bengali painters Abanendranath Tagore and Nandlal Bose are at the pinnacle of modern art in India.

Bengal was ahead of other parts of India in industry and the development of infrastructure. Dwarkanath Tagore set-up indigo factories and sugar plantations; he also prospered in spinning and ship-building industries. Calcutta had soon become the industrial hub of India. Banking and insurance companies were set-up in Bengal. River Steam Navigation was a roaring success. Swadeshi industries in textiles, and pharmaceuticals were set-up and prospered with the fortunes of the freedom movement and the ambition to use India made products. Bipin Chander Pal forestalled Gandhi in 1916 when he advocated passive resistance and the use of India made products. Bengal discovered the tool of boycott which brought freedom nearer. Cobblers of Bengal refused to repair British made shoes. Large scale shoe manufacture was set up in Calcutta which is a leading exporter of shoes. Marwari immigrants into Bengal have given further impetus to industrialization. Calcutta is still in the front rank of Indian industrial centres. J.C. Ghosh organised batches of Indian students for training in advanced industrial technology in Europe and England. The process is still continuing, only, the traffic is both ways now.

Bengal had been an exporter of Indian handicrafts and textiles from ancient times. With independence the potters and weavers of Bengal lead in their crafts. Recent works of Bengal arts and crafts are in great demand by museums and art lovers of the world.

6.5 Bishnupur and Murshidabad

Any mention of arts and crafts of Bengal reminds one of the contribution of Bishnupur's craftsmen. Bishnupur has had the distinction of being the seat of government of semi-independent kings continuously from the seventh century to the 19th century when the last Malla king decided to give up the kingship of his country since people loved riches more and he could get a good price for his claims from the seths of Bardhman. He was fed up with the yearly raids and demands of the Marathas. The kings of Bishnupur must have been adepts in state craft to remain un-submerged during the expansion of Afghan and Mughal power. The Bengal native civilization could develop and blossom in the Malla kingdom for a thousand years untouched by strife. The Malla line was enriched by famous Bagdi rulers Hambir, his son and grandson in the 17th century who were also great builders and had become Vaishnavas. The Bagdi tribe was the first to accept Adi-Malla as their chief in the 8th century. Hambir composed Vaishnava lyrics. Shah Shuja the viceroy appointed by the Delhi emperor had confirmed the Malla rulers in their kingdom. The 17th and 18th centuries saw intense adornment of Bishnupur region with temples. The earliest being the Malleswara Siva temple. The special feature of these temples is the extensive use of terracotta bricks arranged to depict scenes from Ramayna, Mahabharata and Puranas. Each brick is a work of art. The terracotta pictorial art jumped from temple walls to the looms of Bishnupur weavers of saris. The famous Baluchari saris from the nearby village of Baluchar are collector items all over the world. Bishnupur has led in miniature painting, giving rise to the Murshidabad school of painting. Bishnupur classical music was adopted as a mode of worship by the 10th century renaissance leaders of Hindu religion.

All the well known style of temple architecture are illustrated in a compact region in Bishnupur. *The Marg* magazine (March 2003) has published beautiful pictures of various Bishnupur temples. Many artists, musicians and intellectuals either hail from Bishnupur or have spent their formative years there. Below are given the names of various temples that illustrate some of the Bengal styles of temple architecture. The basic structure is like that of the Bengal hut with one or more *chala* (roof). Some of the important temples are : Malleswara temple, Keshava Raya temple (Deul type), Siddhesvara temple of Bahudara (Nagara style), Radha Binod temple (At-Chala), Jor Bangla or Kasht Raya temple (Chala type Bangla temple), Kalachand temple (Ratna style), Madan Mohan temple (Ek Ratna); another important temple is Krishna-Balram temple. An impressive structure is the Ras Manch, where the deities from the region paid court to Lord Krishna.

Murshidabad declined in its glory after the Nawab's defeat at Plassey and the shift of all trappings of power to Calcutta (now Kolkata) the seat of East India Company. Still, Murshidabad continued to flourish well into the 19th century and reminded Bengal of Gaur; the ancient capital city of Bengal. The founder and other potentates of Murshidabad have built many famous mosques there, viz. Katra mosque built by Mir Qasim, and the Chowk Mosque. Another impressive building from the 10th century is the Hazardwari palace of thousand doors in European style. Opposite the city palace is the Imambara built by the founder (architect being one Sadiq Ali). Mahomet's foot print was also set-up when brought from Arabia and Gaur, but it has now been transferred back to Gaur. Murshidabad was well known for pleasure spots for the rich Nabobs, Moti Jhil being one such pleasure spot.

Murshidabad became a centre for painting (later Mughal style). An eminent Murshidabad painter was Deep Chand. An important subject of painting was paintings depicting various Ragas. Three famous albums are in existence from those days and show painter's interest in music. Ivory carving became legendary. Luxury boats were made for the nabobs and replicas in ivory are to be seen in various collections. Tulsi Karigar, an ivory carver of Murshidabad was invited by the Jaipur court and honoured by the Nawab on his return.

Murshidabad cottons were the source of wealth of Bengal and the European trading companies. Many Marwari families attracted by the textile trade of Murshidabad later became art collectors. Fateh Chand a famous trader was awarded the title of Jagat Seth by the Nawab and he was the banker to Bengal including the East India Company. The Neminath temple or a typical Jain mansion are the symbols of Jain wealth and munificence in that city.

7

East India Company

On seeing the riches flowing into Holland and Portugal, the British also floated their East India Company with exclusive trading rights with the east. They first operated from Hooghly and then from Calcutta, now re-named Kolkata. Their trade had Indian headquarters in Madras (Chennai) and they had a branch operating at Bombay, now re-named Mumbai. There was virtually anarchy in Bengal after the death of Aurangzeb, the Mughal emperor in the Deccan. In Madras too, there was dispute among claimants to the Arcot throne. One faction had alliance with French garrison developed to guard French trading interests in India. The British also desired to fish in the troubled waters there. The British won on setting their ally the Nawab of Arcot on the throne at Arcot through the wise moves and valour of their clerk Clive. Clive was then sent to Calcutta to rescue the British interests which were sorely beset by the Bengal ruler Shuja-ud-Daula, the Mughal governor with his seat of government at Murshidabad, whose demands of money from the British company were constantly rising. The king at Delhi, the governor as well as the foreign merchants were at the mercy of the marauding Marathas.

Clive after studying the situation seems to have decided to have a more pliant Nawab at Murshidabad. The Nawab was served by self-seeking grandees who were open to sell themselves to highest bidder. Clive purchased the subversion of Mir Jaffar, the Nawab's heir and his commander-in-chief. Clive was to force a war on the Nawab and Mir Jaffar will desert the Nawab on the field of battle. He was assured of immediate accession to the throne once the victory was of the conspirators. Events happened as planned and the Battle of Plassey which was never a battle gave the supreme authority to

Clive in Bengal after the new Nawab had also nominally submitted to the emperor at Delhi along with a large present from the Bengal treasury. As a price of help rendered to Mir Jaffar, the East India Company got the right to pursue trade and commerce in Bengal and to collect revenue for the Nawab's treasury from his subjects. The company officials could coerce the subjects any amount and the blame will be placed at the door of the Nawab. The company became rich beyond imagination by legitimate revenue collection and legitimate trade profits from tax exemption and monopolies granted by the government in the pocket of the company. Bengal suffered double loss because most European employees of the company carried on trade on the side for personal profit under the company's banner. Soon the company could purchase from the imperial court at Delhi, the royal appointment of revenue collector for Bengal, Bihar and Orissa.

The Muslims had a lot more to bewail. Suddenly the avenue of employment in the army was cut off. The company regarded Muslim loyalty with suspicion. The Sanyasi and Farazi revolts were primarily peasant uprisings, but the peasants were mostly Muslim and were led by Muslim mullahs. The weavers, most of whom were Muslim also suffered terribly because of the company policy to import cloth from U.K. In 1793, rural police was disbanded, thus shutting off another avenue of employment for the rural Muslims. There was heavy handed gumashta collections from the peasants mostly Muslim. The landed gentry was replaced by absentee landlords, mostly Hindu who employed gumashtas to represent them and to collect taxes and extra levies from the peasants. In order to squeeze and loot the peasants, new landlords often protected and raised robber gangs. The Muslims devised the desperate slogan "Jihad or Hijrat", i.e. holy war or migrate to Muslim kingdoms. It was this very ill-advised slogan that was raised by Indian Muslims in certain Indian states where Muslims were inconsequential in numbers.

When later, the company devised the system of subsidiary alliances, they became the master of many Indian states. The device was an improvement over the *Chauth* extracted by the Marathas. The company started annexing some states or their part when they settled the disputes that always erupted at the time of succession of a new ruler. The company also befriended the Indian financiers by helping them become richer through crumbs from their monopolistic trade in certain commodities. They also created a loyal, new land owning gentry by allowing rich zamindars to enlarge their estates at the cost of the cultivators. The public was pitilessly ground down by the company with its feudal authority for the collection of taxes, monopolies and also insatiable greed and mutual gratification with the Indian figure-heads who made no contribution to the generation of capital. Before the battle of Plassey, the gold and bullion was flowing into India from the European trade. Later there are mind boggling figures of wealth that went out to England through the company or its employees and agents. When Mir Jaffar tried to plug the drain on the country's riches, he was also deposed and Mir Qasim was made the Nawab. The English company kept up its practices till the victory at Buxar where they gained similar control over Oudh, the richest state in the imperial domains.

The company administered areas like that of Calcutta became an oasis of peace in the whole of India, assured from the ravages of both the company and the Marathas or the non-existent administrative acumen of the Mughal authority. Fifty years after the battle of Plassey, the East India Company was controlling the Delhi emperor and thus whole of India and waging wars with the Maratha chiefs, the Nizam and Tipu Sultan of Mysore and winning over them one by one in one-sided alliance with others. If the company forces lost a battle, they were tenacious enough to come back for next till they were successful. The Englishmen of the company had a vision of greatness of England and assumed a sense of moral superiority which they lost only when Mahatma Gandhi waged his struggle for liberation of India and of all European colonies from a pedestal of moral strength from basic standards of civilization. To secure their domains in India the company subdued Assam, Punjab, and Mirs and Pirs of Sind and of western frontiers from Peshawar to Quetta. They spread a network of railways, postal services, inspection houses for their bureaucrats, and hill stations for the families of Europeans. They also brought in Missionary societies to spread new education and hospitals and to proselytize Indians into Christianity through their religious zeal.

The company policies were designed to exploit and despoil India of wealth in every way. They had mastered the art and craft of colonial government, by keeping up the image of neutrality and justice for internal complaints of Indians but consistently laboured to impart better status to Europeans in India superior to Indians in the matter of pay etc. for same work and only a trickle of Indians were either qualified or permitted to take up positions of greater authority which were reserved for the Europeans. This policy as well as atrocities on the Indian ruling houses ultimately estranged the company soldiers which were largely Indian sepoys from Bengal and Madras. This was the genesis of the sepoy mutiny of 1857 which started in Bengal and when it failed brought about changes in government and its policies in the interest of the imperial ambitions. Indian superior technology or industry was either thwarted or stolen till by the end of 19th century form a position of being the workshop of the world. India was importing needles and road rollers from Great Britain. The company rule ended in 1857 and British Parliament became the arbiter of Indian official decisions and policies. Many reforms were carried out during the company rule like abolition of child marriages, suppression of Sati, thugee, Pindari loot, and equality of all Indians in law and generally people realised that the English could give them the rule of law which they never got from earlier despots. The initial wealth and knowledge that the company and European traders brought to India had foremost impact in Bengal and Bengal naturally became the leader of reformation of Indian religions and society. Modern banking and industry, shipping or steel production started in Bengal. The Bengal Hindus took to English liberal education like duck to water and produced poets and writers of the calibre of Tagore or Nirad Chaudhuri. The period 1757-1857 was the EIC-cum-Bengali century of India. Indian centres for education and industry developed at Bombay, Madras, and Lahore to the extent these suited the British system in India. Western education became entrenched and the futile experiments with Hindi and Urdu failed for higher education. The use of the English language spread to all fields particularly engineering, management and medicine and is continuously expanding so much so that even the rural population is asking for English medium schools.

The company rule in India was a big change agent and the changes had far reaching effects for India and the world. Many modern institutions particularly the Asiatic Society, various surveys and explorations, archaeology and European expert attention to Sanskrit and ancient Indian advances in philosophy and medicine etc. were begun. As the company ruled territory expanded, better communications dictated primarily by military need also opened rural India to modernization. The rule of law and internal order became normal but for the exploitation by the British in alliance with the educated and the rich of India.

Bengal had hardly any respite from constant warfare between intruders and claimants to Bengal kingdom. Only the East India Company of the British showed some concern for the rule of law for its subjects so long as there was no diminution of company income. A semblance of good government and secular justice for the subjects brought an increase in trade and revenues of the company. Imparting of science and education in English and no religious bias against the employment of Hindus coupled with natural bent of Indians for science and technology opened the flood gates of enthusiasm and capability of the Bengalis for advancement. The European companies were the change agents. There was sudden upsurge of community structures and renaissance in Hindus and later among Muslims too. The Hindus especially rediscovered themselves on the coat tails of the European scholarship. The ancient fairs of Bengal carried the message of awakening, secularism and self-help, and later to Hindu-Muslim unity and national struggles against despots and intruders as well as the British. The message was for all castes and creeds especially when the common Bengali had been brought together by the Vaishnava movement and vibrant Sufi doctrines of equality and love in the eyes of God.

The district of Hooghly close to Calcutta became most advanced in education and cultural pursuits. The Portuguese had settled in Hooghly as early as 1535 A.D. The Christian Missions by boldly attacking superstition and caste high-handedness among the people contributed greatly. The Bandel Church and monastery were built by the Goa friars in 1593. The Baptist missionary society was formed in 1793. Important places of pilgrimage, like Tribeni, Guptapara, Tarakeswar, and Chinsura and the principal festivals like Makar Sankranti in March, Vishnupadi Sankranti in winter and the great bathing festival in spring became conduits of awakening. According to tradition, Jafar Khan (whose tomb is a specimen of Muslim epigraphy) worshipped Ganga. One Mahesh was miraculously enriched and he is part of the Satyanarayana legend popular both among the Hindus and the Muslims of Bengal. Guptapara became a centre of Sanskrit learning. Dara Ghazi of Tripurà, a scholar of Sanskrit became an admirer of Hinduism. He has also been identified with Jafar Khan who had a mosque built at Tribeni for Muslim pilgrims. There was considerable fellow feeling among the holy people of all communities.

From ancient times the poor had been ground down by forced labour or forced levies. In general, the British, even their armies on the march spared undue hardship to the public. Indian lawyers could argue for their clients even in highest company court which enforced English law. Many Bengal lawyers and professionals became rich and famous. Most Indian leaders preferred western education.

8

Renaissance and National Consciousness Begins in Bengal

Attacks on Hindu temple cities, theocratic rule at Delhi, oppression of Hindu subjects in many Muslim kingdoms, expressed or silent Hindu anger could never make an Indian nation. India had in the past defeated the invading Greek, Kushan and Hoon contingents and then by fair treatment and give and take in religion and philosophy assimilated them. In spite of bravery of Indian individuals and sacrifices, they never united sufficiently to convincingly defeat the invading Muslim forces who came with the expressed purpose of converting non-Muslims to Islam and to destroy any independent Hindu kingdoms. The local bravery could bring about only a share in power for the Rajputs and with time the aggressive zeal of Muslims evaporated except its rebirth under imperial midwifery in Muslims of certain border areas. The spontaneous unity of dispossessed Hindu and Muslim kingdoms during the 1857 mutiny, and the acceptance by all of the figurehead emperor at Delhi coupled with the aggression of Marathas on all who thwarted them in search of loot from all Indian kingdoms brought about a closing of ranks of common people, both Hindu or Muslim.

In India the Indian way of life gave equal recognition to all modes of worship and there was never a chosen religion made a state religion excepting for some intervals by the Delhi Sultanate. There was considerable give and take regarding religion and philosophy. The Sanatan Dharma of the majority of the population found ways to integrate with Muslims through common fairs and festivals, mutual respect and forbearance and the understanding that humanism is the aim of all religion and philosophy. Equal rights and equality in law is the prerequisite for the formation of a nation. Casteism cannot go beyond the village boundaries. The presence of European traders in the coastal areas brought home to the common man the pernicious in-fighting and inequality in Indian society of all hues. The cash in-flow was only from trade which soon became almost a monopoly of the British East India Company. They soon wrested political power from the Mughals and had brought about a new land gentry and a capitalist class cooperating with them in every way. In the company controlled areas soon covering areas from Calcutta to Kanpur, there was rule of law (except that Europeans had exclusive rights), but for Indians, there was a breath of freedom from despots of Indian origin. It took few generations of Englishmen who contributed blood and toil to convince the public that they were going to build an India where lawlessness would be banished. The productivity of Indian industry, agriculture and forests was enough to fill the coffers of the whole world. India had again become the goose that lays the golden egg. Now the British turned to slaughter the goose. They now wished to turn India into a client colony with no technology and no industry or direct trade overseas. The liberal education and Christian missions opened the eyes of Indians to the mistreatment of lower castes when they actually became a lower caste to the Europeans. The European scholars (British, German and French) uncovered the forgotten past and recognized greatness of the ancient Indian civilization now lying neglected under the ruins of their ancient temples and libraries. A thousand years of neglect and destruction of patrons of Hindu arts, combined with the loss of court patronage had brought Indian developments in science and technology practically to a stand-still. The European wealth for the purchase of Indian products gave India a new confidence and subsequent canard raised by the rulers that India could not manufacture anything for even their own use re-kindled pride in swadeshi products and Bengal was the first to experiment with the boycott of western goods that became a potent tool for the liberation of India. Bengal public, especially the Hindus took to western education, British style of life and reformist point of view regarding many defects in Indian practices and superstitions. Raja Ram Mohun Roy was in the forefront of this movement. He propagated his reformist ideas through his weeklies and through the establishment of the Brahmo Samaj. He was particularly active in the demand for the prohibition of *sati* and for allowing widow re-marriage. He was ably supported by many Bengali educated and learned men and women. The young Bengal movement led by De Rozario was a great source of reformist energy so much so that there was a reaction that the youth was plumping for conversion to Christianity, but soon this was found incorrect. It was only experimentation by the youth of Bengal with the western modes of life. They persisted also in their pride for the high reaches of Indian knowledge and technology. A press was started in Calcutta. The Indian newspapers and magazines played a vigorous role in the renaissance of literature and poetry as well as in the reformist endeavours.

From ancient times the poor had been ground down by forced labour or forced levies. In general, the British, even their armies on the march spared undue hardship to the public. Indian lawyers could argue for the clients even in highest company court which enforced English law. Many Bengal lawyers and professionals became rich and famous. Most Indian leaders preferred western education, though they continued to hope that Sanskrit and Persian scholarship would continue to flourish in India. The administration of company territories was taken up directly by the Crown in 1857 after the suppression of the sepoy mutiny. The capital was shifted in 1911 to Delhi from Calcutta and the king of England was crowned the emperor of India at Delhi in 1911. The industrial and commercial capital continued to be Calcutta which lost to Mumbai this status, only after the world war and communal uprisings and famine in Bengal. In 1911 it looked like the British connection would last for ever, as India and Britain seemed to need each other so much. The growing national unity in Bengal was upset first in 1905 when the British partitioned Bengal. This produced the revolutionary movement in India and even when the partition was cancelled, the revolutionary sentiment stayed on and gave the Indian freedom struggle, the first batch of revolutionary leaders who shaped the lives of even the succeeding non-violent revolutionaries. British started treating India as a nation so long as all power stayed with the British government in London. British financial gain from India increased every year.

Indian foreign policy was coined in London. India also joined the war against Germany in 1914. Even Mahatma Gandhi wanted

India to exert for British victory expecting good advancement of India towards self-rule after allied victory. The story of further alienation of India and its non-violent victory against the empire is well known. In the beginning of the 18th century, the Indian society had reached the lowest ebb in its fortunes. Bengal needed to revise its self-image and face reality. The European trading companies acted as change agents. As the company administered areas expanded, there was an upsurge of construction of churches, temples and mosques, as well as schools and industries. The fairs of Bengal contributed now to the spread of well-being to the neglected castes and to the outcastes. Constructive work was started by the educated youth of Bengal after seeing the activities of the missionaries and some government civil service officers often filled with reformist zeal and some capitalists with altruistic frame of mind.

The Portuguese colonialists demonstrated better agricultural practices and introduced the cultivation of tobacco, potato, papaya and pine-apple in Bengal. Charnock founded mercantile Calcutta in 1690. Hindu college was established in 1817. There were already changes in Bengali manners and literature. Macauley with the support of Indian opinion introduced English as the medium of instruction for all advanced learning in 1835. No high level Indian educational conference has made any bold time-bound frame for undoing this. Indians continue to cherish English for science, medicine and management studies. So far experiments with Hindi or Urdu have failed. Thus was begun the renaissance of Indian learning by stalwarts like Vidyasagar, Madhu Sudan Datta, Bankim Chandra Chatterji, Rabindranath Tagore and others. The young Bengal interacted in promoting new reforms under the inspired leadership of young De Rozario who in his brief life of thirty-two years led a band of school-mates to set the Hindu mind on reform and clear thinking following Bacon, Hume and Paine. Humanism and secularism was foremost in Bengal mind at that stage. The Europeans started plantations of tea, jute, pine-apple etc. Private enterprise began the development of the country and the infrastructure to support the enhanced trading and exports. The British companies embarked on expanding the rail and road network. The English Company standardized weights and measures. Indian industry was reluctantly allowed to grow. Its value to the empire was fully utilized in the First World War. Urbanization grew around markets. India awoke from slumber and saw the havoc brought about by feudal struggles for exploiting the poor of the land. The 19th century was also the century of social change. Benthemite literature prevailed.

Ishwar Chandra Gupta (1812-1859) led the liberation from the shackles of pornographic Shakta Padavalis. The Bengalis also became aware that proper traditionalism was superior to the western philosophy. Tagore was the leader of the critical appreciation of Indian traditional philosophy when free from taboos, and of Indian aesthetics. Hinduism was getting rid of unnecessary rituals and was bent on women's emancipation. The English were sympathetic to the new face of Hinduism and later they would first be neutral towards all reform and later antagonists smelling rebellion in reform and national unity. The national song "Bande Matram" was composed in 1870. Bankim Lahiri publicly discarded the sacred thread. He attacked the judicial impunity of Europeans. The English daily *Bande Matram* was started in 1906, actively propagating rebellion and freedom from British bondage. A weekly "*Sudhakar*" supported partition of Bengal for greater attention to the down-trodden Muslim peasantry of east Bengal. "*Ahmedi*" (1896) worked for Hindu-Muslim unity for freedom which reached a high pitch just before the poison of separate electorates was injected into the political mind of Indians in 1919 and again boosted in 1935. The British attacked growing unity, by the partitioning of Bengal in 1905, which was vehemently resisted by the revolutionary sentiment in Bengal and withdrawn by government in 1911, but the British resolved from then on to further brain-wash the minorities for seeking separate identity from the Hindus, only the tenacity of Mahatma Gandhi and the strength of the Indian National Congress spearheading the freedom struggle supported by nationalist Muslims and nationalist following in other sections of society saved India from complete balkanization. India had to yield to a truncated Pakistan to the Muslim League, the demand had been planted and nourished by the British and their communist war allies. It was gustily taken up by the chauvinist mullahs dreaming of the Muslim conquest of the world. (This Islamic agenda is now in the open through global terrorism.)

The Bengali intellectual has been in the forefront of revival of arts and crafts or of industrialization. Girish Chander Ghosh was the founder of the national theatre. Dr. Mohinderlal Sarkar founded the Bengal Science Association in 1867. The Indian Association for the cultivation of science was established in 1870. Sir C.V. Raman carried out his Nobel prize winning researches in the Association laboratories in Calcutta. Scientific contributions of Sir J.C. Bose, Acharya Profulla Chandra Roy, Dr. S.N. Bose are world famous. The multi-dimensional personality of the Nobel laureate Rabindranath Tagore is dear to every Indian. He was poet, philosopher, composer, essayist, novelist, actor, playwright and a constructive worker besides being an educationist of Vishwa Bharati fame. The Indian national anthem is one of Tagore's songs composed well ahead of the establishment of the Indian Republic and one of his songs has become the national anthem of Bangladesh. The Bengali painters Abanindranath Tagore and Nandlal Bose were the pioneers of modern art in India. Dwarkanath Tagore established indigo factory in India, besides sugar plantations and also prospered in spinning and ship building industries. Banking and insurance companies were established in Calcutta. His River Navigation Company was a roaring success. The indigenous manufacture of textiles, pharmaceuticals was set up. Bipin Chander Pal forestalled Mahatma Gandhi in advocating passive resistance and use of "made in India" goods in the struggle for Indian freedom. (The cobblers of Calcutta refused to repair British manufactured shoes). J.C. Ghosh organized batches of Indian students to go abroad to learn industrial manufacture. Now every Indian is keen to garnish new knowledge overseas and place it when required at the service of the mother-land. The resurgence of Indian classical learning started with important contributions from European scholars. Sir William Hunter wrote "The Indian Mind" in 1870 and "Defence of Hindu Theism" in 1887. He wrote also "Monotheism of the Vedas". His journal, the Bengal Herald was published in Persian, Bengali and English. Madame Blavatsky made India proud when she showed her convincing preference for Indian philosophy. She set up the Hindu school at Banaras which later blossomed into the Banaras Hindu University. She set up Theosophical lodges in India and abroad claiming to derive all scientific knowledge by meditation alone.

8.1 Growth of Press and of Unrest

The Bengali century (1757-1857) saw publication of many newspapers and journals. The press was fearless and often critical of company's policies and actions. East India Company staff was not creating a welfare state but was there to make profits for the British shareholders of the company. They were still responsive to the British public opinion and the press tried to reflect this opinion in India. The Englishmen in India held firmly to the opinion that they were superior to Indians in religion, philosophy and good government and assumed moral superiority irrespective of actual ethics of their actions which would be justified only by commercial or military necessity. They held also that everyone was equal before law. This was quite a welcome departure from the environment of perpetual inequality in India. In 1875, there were 478 newspapers in the company controlled territories. The writings of Deenabandhu, Harishchandra Bannerjee, Naved Chandra Sen, R.C. Datta, Tagore, B.C. Chatterjee were soul stirring. The period 1875-1884 has been dubbed as the seed time of Indian independence. The company got a jolt from the protest of the educated Bengalis on their attempt to enact the Ilbert bill for separate court procedure for the European defaulters requiring only English judges to sit in judgement. The rebellious press forced the company to withdraw this bill. The company partitioned Bengal in 1905 in order to reduce the influence of educated Bengalis of the Calcutta region on the peasant masses of East Bengal. The British now wanted first to brainwash the Muslim majority of East Bengal to fear the rule of the educated classes mainly Hindu. The educated Hindu as well as Muslim stood united against the 1905 partition which had to be annulled in 1911. The British prepared for the partition brought about in 1947 by slowly injecting the poison of separate electorates first begun from the stage managed petition of a Muslim deputation from Bengal led by Aga Khan. The moderates among the educated Indians believed in the continuation of the British power as they sincerely felt they were the best educators. The European scholars had discovered and brought before the public in translation, the riches of the Sanskrit heritage. Certain government actions particularly irked the Indians and the effect was cumulative. This was ably aired by the revolutionary teachings of Bankim Chandra Chaterjee, Ramakrishna

Paramhans, and Raj Narain Bose. The company imposed some restrictions on the recruitment of educated Bengalis and later on Hindus in general on the basis of their being over represented in government services when over the years they were doing all the leg work for the British for the administration of the country. When there was the rebellious call of Gandhi for the British to quit India and general repression of Congress-men throughout India resulted, it was parts of Bengal that temporarily threw off the British yoke and occupied the collectorates and police stations.

The government had no clear-cut policy of development or relief from frequent food and water problems of scarcity or of floods. Every famine led to thousands of starvation deaths, beggary and overcrowding of cities. The Christian missions who were seen in peacetime quite hob-nobbing with the British, acted as good samaritans and undertook care of orphans after every famine. This was however misunderstood as an effort to increase the numbers of the Christian community in India which was expected to be more loyal to the imperialists. This was evidently a misunderstanding. When eventually, India became free, the Christian and other minority communities stayed on in India, only few individuals preferred to go to foreign lands and many of them have regretted that move. Major famines visited Bengal in 1837, 1875, and 1947. Bengal was repeatedly thrown in chaos.

Bengal was active in Congress directed direct action movements especially in 1929, they led in the non-cooperation movement. They were second to none in the boycott of foreign goods and courts. They took to hand spinning. A Bengal national university was established. C.R. Das and other Bengal leaders in Congress proposed to enter legislatures in order to fully project their non-cooperation. They formed a distinct Swaraj party in 1932. The *satyagrah* movement was active in Bengal against the forest laws and faced a reign of terror in Midnapore. The Gagging Act or the Vernacular Press Act of 1908 was enforced after the start of the non-cooperation movement and many publications had to cease work and lose security etc. as well as suffer other punitive action.

Agrarian unrest was natural when the peasants were facing oppression. There was a sustained strike from indigo cultivators in 1859-60. The European planters were driving the peasants as serfs under the lash. The Nila Darpan play by Dinabandhu Mitra shows the plight of the cultivators vividly. James Long, a missionary wrote a factual pamphlet that created an uproar in Britain. Agrarian unrest spread to east Bengal in 1870. The Champaran agrarian unrest was enquired into by Gandhi himself. Such unrests led to the Naxalite movement led by an extremist communist faction in 1962 that is still continuing in certain areas of Telengana (Andhra) where the Hyderabad state police killed 4000-rebels before Hyderabad became a part of free India. In spite of Gandhi inspired Vinoba Bhave's benevolent trustee movement and Bhoodan or land gifted to the land-less, the peasants still have to be made secure in reality regarding their ownership of land and their proper wages.

The economic backwardness came under young Bengal's scrutiny. Raj Narain started the Jatiya Gaurav Sampada Sabha. All India conferences were organized in 1883 and 1885, precursors of National Congress set up in 1889. The coinage of the Indian states was brought in line with the one in use in British Indian provinces. Commercialization of agriculture was begun. Many mills were started around Calcutta. Coal mining industry was established around Asansol and Burdwan. The Bengal National Chamber of Commerce started functioning from 1887. Calcutta public library was started in 1831. (Now the use of the internet is penetrating schools and colleges all over India.) The society started looking down on self-torture as a mark of religious fervour or on the lack of attention to the old persons left to die unattended on the banks of the Ganges (Antaranjali). The demonstrated secular approach to worship by Sri Ramakrishna and the eloquence of his disciple Vivekananda have mapped afresh the religious goals of Indian thinking those of secularism, humanism and patriotism.

9

Revolutionary Movements in Bengal

Bengal had suffered a lot in their fight for justice during the company regime. The list of suppressed rebellions is appalling : Darbhanga uprising 1769-1774, Bishnupur rebellion 1770, Cham rebellion, Manbhum, Bankura district 1777, Sylhet insurgency 1799, Haji Farazi insurgency 1828-1847 and Dadu Mian uprising sparked by the exploitation of peasants by indigo planters, Santhal revolt 1855-1856, Titu Mir uprising, Barisal 1831, Wahabi uprising, Twenty-four Parganas and Nadia 1832, Pagal Panthi uprising of Mymensingh 1833, Mangal Singh Pandey blown by Cannon in front of Bengal company of sepoys that led to mutiny of 1857. (One may also add Bengali sailors mutiny on board Royal Indian Navy vessel off Bombay 1945, which was the last straw on the back of British imperialism in India after the exploits of the Indian National Army led by Subhas Chandra Bose that attacked and won a large area in East India upto Kohima after occupying Andaman Islands with the help of the Japanese naval forces and entering India from Burma). Violent rebellions started spontaneously in Bengal when the suffering became acute with no redress visible. In order to safeguard their own interests the British decided to partition Bengal because of the reformist clamour mounting among intelligentsia around Calcutta. The partition of Bengal was opposed in every way and eventually it was cancelled. From the experience of the successful struggle, the revolutionaries gained confidence and Bengal became the home of many terrorists fighting with guns for the liberation of India. As a means of suppression of the terrorists, the government instituted court cases against the terrorists caught in their net, or against their vociferous supporters. One such court case was against a crowd of revolutionaries involved in the

Chittagong armoury raid. The Andaman cellular prison was the place of incarceration of many Bengali patriots. Rash Behari Bose threw a bomb on the Viceroy Lord Harding when he was entering ceremonially Delhi on an elephant. Subhas Chandra Bose was influenced by the philosophy and sacrifices of the terrorists when he wanted the Congress to start an armed struggle during the world war. The exploits of his national army based on volunteers released from prisoners of war in the Japanese prison camps after the initial victories over the British imperial forces in Burma and Singapore. Neta Ji had a clearer vision of Indian unity and had demonstrated the communal amity prevailing in the Azad Hind Fauj (INA) and in the liberated areas. Though the Congress gained some mileage on account of the struggle of the Azad Hind Fauj and the spirited defence by the Congress leaders like Jawaharlal Nehru of the imprisoned fauj captains captured by the British, yet there was a disappointment that there was no general uprising in the country. According to Bose who invited such an uprising, India would have remained united in victory over the British control of India. India could get only a negotiated settlement and freedom cost us a lot. India was partitioned and a potential enemy was created in the form of Pakistan over the protests of large mass of Muslims led by Khan Abdul Gaffar Khan or nationalist Muslim leadership of Sind, Kashmir and Balochistan. Out of these only Jammu and Kashmir state could be salvaged by the Congress and the state nationalist Muslim leadership. Pakistan of partitioned India included East Bengal, for long the goal of imperial policy was to rescue the Muslim cultivators from the virus of independence and reform prevailing in West Bengal. This policy had received a set back when the earlier partitioning of Bengal was not allowed to occur by the nationalists of Bengal. Now the imperialists had honed their policy of divide and rule further.

Violent revolutionary movements had been natural in the environment of Bengal. Each fort had a band of marauders officially armed to collect the revenue for the emperor but actually to exploit the poor. During the struggle for freedom Bengal was the home of most of the violent freedom fighters. Their policy was to hold secret parleys and collect members and cash by all means particularly by looting government funds. They would also endeavour to punish particularly obnoxious government agents and informers taking their cue from the freedom struggles of Ireland and Italy. We have already referred to the Chittagong armoury raid or the wounding of the viceroy by having bomb thrown at him. Many terrorists suffered life imprisonment in the Andamans or suffered hanging on the gallows. Kakori train robbery was one of the classical happenings and very suicidal for the terrorists since the British could extract confessions from some prisoners and they got many rebellious leaders implicated in the case, who could be imprisoned or banished. Jatindernath Das scarificed his life by hunger strike for better treatment of revolutionaries in prisons. The famous leaders who could find haven abroad included Bhai Permanand, Rash Behari Bose, and Shri Aurbindo Ghosh. The terrorists included Bhagat Singh and his young companions who climbed the gallows with patriotic fervour. On the realization of freedom, certain leaders were not happy with Gandhi-Nehru leadership and propagated Stalin or Mao type dictatorship under the aegis of the Indian Communist party. A faction is in perpetual rebellion on the east coastal region of Orissa under the banner of People's War Group, while most of the states of India elected Congress-men to the state legislatures. Same has been happening in Kerala, the state most advanced in education. The Communists would like to curtail the strengthening of the centre *vis-á-vis* autonomous functioning of various states.

The sacrifices made by the revolutionaries had great influence on the people of India. Mahatma Gandhi called them great patriots. He however argued that the English government in India rested on the co-operation it receives from India. If this cooperation is withheld, the government will come to a standstill. Bipin Chander Pal had already analysed the situation the same way. The Congress was inclined to the non-violent mass movement proposed by Gandhi. Violent movement by few conspirators could always be snuffed out at an early stage. Indian freedom should not only make Indians free from the yoke of British slavery but also free them from age-long tyranny of caste Hindus on the majority of lower castes and free the Indian society of repugnant features like untouchability and child marriages etc. The programme adopted therefore was of reform in society along with mass disobedience and non-cooperation.

Mahatma Gandhi was master of strategy and tactics. He made

communal amity as one of the important planks of his freedom movement. The limited success in this arena brought about a limited success to the freedom movement. The boycott of imported goods and setting up of Indian manufactures was another important plank. There were bonfires of imported cloth all over the country. In order to befriend the Muslims, the Congress made common cause with the Muslim demand to have the Caliph continue after the First World War. But there was revolutionary mood in the Turkish Islam under the leadership of Kemal Ataturk and the Muslims there repudiated the office of the Caliph. The British had long ago realized that the unity of Hindus and Muslims of India spelled doom for their hold over the Indian empire. The scenes of fraternization during the Khilafat agitation alerted them for strengthening their divide and rule policy. They granted special loan to a Muslim leader of Bengal to bolster the organization of the Muslim League in Bengal. The Aga Khan a pensioner of Great Britain and self-appointed representative of Indian Muslims petitioned the viceroy for the grant of separate electorates and reservation of all posts for Muslims in proportion to their relative numbers. The British held three round table conferences in London and wanted separate electorates for all religious minorities including the scheduled castes of the Hindus. Ambedkar, the recognized leader of scheduled castes cast his weight in favour of retention of joint electorates for the scheduled castes in the Hindu fold in order to save the life of Mahatma Gandhi who had gone on hunger strike on this issue. Later many scheduled caste members followed Ambedkar to become converted to Buddhism. (Ambedkar was recognized by the Buddhists as a Bodhisattva and his statue could now be enshrined in Buddhist temples for worship). Jinnah, the leader of the Muslim league continued to propagate Muslims being a separate nation from the Hindu nation living in India and stuck to his demand for a Muslim homeland carved out of India when the British relinquished their control. In Bengal the Krishak Praja party was stronger than Muslim League, but their government was dismissed as in other Muslim majority provinces. The Muslim League staged violent communal riots and attempted ethnic cleaning of East Bengal by outright killing and looting of Hindu residents. The carnage was stopped by the joint efforts of Mahatma Gandhi and Suhravardy, the former elected chief minister of Bengal. The communal riots of 1946 just after the ravages of the man made famine there in 1942 just about broke the spirit of "no partition" faction of Bengal.

Radicalism has been endemic to Bengal. At the time of Vedic supremacy in the rest of country, Bengal took to Buddhism. Later it went all out for Jainism or gave ear to the spread of Islam. The interplay of various religions finally gave the Bengalis their own universal religion of Sri Ramakrishna and Vivekananda where all philosophies co-exist. At the name of Sri Ramakrishna, a digression is necessary and Sri Ramakrishna's contribution to the Indian cultural renaissance is explained in Section 9.3. When the rest of the country on the whole favoured democracy and respect of equal human rights of all citizens, Bengal stood out for communism and dictatorship of the proletariat of the Stalin variety. The Naxalites or the extremists favoured Maoism. Even now West Bengal has a communist provincial government which is now willing to cooperate with the Centre in their planned development of India. East Bengal, when Pakistan was rabidly communal, favoured curtailing the rights of non-Muslims even though before independence, Jinnah had imagined a respectable life for minorities in Pakistan. Inside Pakistan, the Muslim League government would not recognize Bengali as a national language. Even when the Bengali leader Mujib-ul-Rehman won a majority in the central legislature of Pakistan, the league refused to recognize him as the future prime minister of Pakistan and with Punjab dominated army tried to keep east Bengal in line with force. There was a civil war and East Pakistan waged a war of liberation from the domination of West Pakistan. Thus was the new nation of Bangladesh formed with the support and recognition from India. There was practically a mutiny of military officers loyal to Pakistan mentality and the new Prime Minister, Mujib was killed by Col. Zia-ul-Rehman, who set up a military dictatorship later confirmed by military run elections as in West Pakistan. But to gain further acceptance in the world, new democratic elections were held in which the Awami League the organization under whose banner Mujib had liberated Bangladesh, again came into power. In the latest election Begum Zia of the Bengal Nationalist party of the slayer of Mujib has come back into power. India and Pakistan are both struggling to favour their favourite leader of Bangladesh. The future of Bangladesh is rather grim for want of industries and want of liberal policies affecting the public.

The communists who happen to be masters of slogans have won elections in West Bengal for quite some time. They continue to warn the peasants against the bourgeois policies of the Centre and paint them as colonialist so far as the eastern part of the country is concerned and continuously flog the petty state nationalists like Mizo, Naga, Bodo and Manipur liberation movements from Bengali grip. Most of the liberators are led and supported by communists of Bengal or two-nation theorists of East Bengal. The Delhi government believing in the national unity, wishes to please all regional aspirations and has created new states to satisfy the self-development efforts in these areas. All the constructive efforts of the Delhi government are dubbed as befooling the public by the communists. Mr. Basu, the communist leader of Bengal when approached to lead the Central government as head of a leftist coalition refused saying that there was not much scope for national reconstruction in the present constitutional environment and the absence of genuine revolution led by communism. Already, the intellectuals of Bengal are fed up with the Naxalite anarchists but they still favour practically full state autonomy bordering on freedom in a lose All India Federation with the right of secession residing with states a la communist theories, but the collapse of multi-state Soviet Union has weakened their arguments, so has the leaning of China towards market economy and globalization. A change in Bengali political ideology is now expected both in east and west Bengal in the next few years after the pacification of local demands in East India.

9.1 Agrarian Unrest in Bengal

Oppressive zamindars with an heartless revenue system was opposed by Dhalburn uprising (1769-1771), Ranghar rebellion (1783) under the leadership of Durjaya Narayan, Bishnupur rebellion in 1770 and Cham rebellion (1777-1779) followed by the semi-religious depredations of Devi Chaudhurani of Santan fame immortalized in *Anand Math.* Sylhet insurgency was intense in 1749 led by Haji Shaukatullah, Santhal rebellion has already been mentioned. There was a general uprising in 24 Parganas under the leadership of Titu and Wahabi Nisar Ali. The Kol rebellion of 1831-32 was against the obstruction imposed on their forest rights. There was a Pagal Panthi uprising in 1844 in Mymensingh. All these uprisings were violently suppressed by Company law makers who later repaired the defective laws or their defective enforcement. The unrest was natural due to periodic famines. Often there was failure of timely rains in successive years. Sometimes there were troubles because of change in the system of collection of revenue. There was lack of policy and mismanagement in the control of prices. The zamindars, moneylenders, lawyers and lambardars combined to exploit the poor uneducated peasants. The peasants of Bengal and Bihar were in the forefront of the final 1942 movement of the Congress after they had passed the Quit India resolution.

9.2 Sacrifices by Bengal Revolutionaries

The Bengal revolutionaries have the pride of place in sacrifices for the extermination of oppressive British officials. Khudiram Bose was hanged for throwing a bomb at Kingford, the Presidency magistrate. Alipore conspiracy case led to searches in Manaktala and imprisonment of many revolutionaries; the approver, Narendra Gosain was killed by fellow prisoners in jail. Asutosh Biswas who had been the prosecutor in the Gosain murder case was killed. Later Rash Behari Bose fled to Japan where he died in 1945 and had the satisfaction of seeing the formation of the INA by Subhas Chandra Bose. Sachindra Sanyal, Ganesh Pingale had prepared for a rebellion all over India by the Ghadar party. The Ghadarites were tried in nine batches. In the Lahore conspiracy case, forty-two persons were sentenced to death, another 114 conspirators were sentenced to transportation and life imprisonment in the Andamans. The revolutionaries believed in counter-terrorism against the terrorism let loose by the government. The revolutionaries were above caste or creed and had single goal of driving out the imperialists. Post-1942 revolutionaries drew inspiration from them as well as the October revolution of the Soviet Union. Bhagat Singh was an ardent admirer of Lenin and sacrificed his life before seeing the Stalinist dictatorial hold over the party in Russia. He was critical of those who obstructed the freedom struggle in the name of one or other religion. An action became well known as the Kakori train dacoity case in which the revolutionaries robbed government treasury being transferred from collection city to the Imperial Bank in a capital city. The revolutionaries, Ashfaque-ullah-Khan, Pandit Ram Prasad Bismil, and Rajendra Lahiri were some of the heroes. As a revenge killing by lathi blows, of Lala Lajpat Rai, when he was leading a massive demonstration against the Simon Commission at Lahore, Bhagat Singh shot and killed the police officer involved. After the surrender of Bhagat Singh at Delhi after exploding a bomb in the assembly chamber which was meant to awaken the legislators to the true state of affairs in the country, he was also tried for this murder and sentenced to death along with his associates Rajguru and Sukhdev. The trio were hanged secretly in Jail and their bodies reduced to ashes on the banks of the Sutlej near Ferozpur. Bhagat Singh, was the intellectual leading the revolutionaries. The sacrifice of Bhagat Singh and his associates ignited countrywide strikes and demonstrations and the awakening was also noticed by Gandhi who admitted that Bhagat Singh's sacrifice would not be in vain. He also protested that the path of violence was inefficient for India's freedom which required a mass movement of civil disobedience, breaking one by one of imposed laws, boycott of British goods and reformation of the Indian society as well as by achieving Hindu-Muslim unity; all these means had already been spelled out and experimented within Bengal. The series of non-violent campaigns and repeated repression of these ultimately led to the fateful quit India resolution of the Congress Working Committee at Bombay in August 1942, calling on the British to quit India, and the Indians to wage a 'do or die' struggle if the British continued their policy of repression. The extent of the non-violent struggles and their repression is vividly summarized by Louis Fisher in the words, "The British beat the Indians; the Indians neither cringed nor complained, nor retreated. This made the Indian invincible."

There was a major mass struggle after August 1942, the most prominent part of the struggle was in Bengal and Bihar where whole districts threw away the yoke of slavery and tasted freedom. The Indian National Army raised by Neta Ji from volunteers among the Prisoner of war camps of Japan and Indian residents in south east Asia attacked India from outside and raced to occupy Indian soil in the Andamans and upto Kohima on the mainland. The British were constrained to release INA officers on spirited defence put up by

Nehru and the wide ranging revolt in the Indian Navy. The British now had a change of heart and of government in U.K. and the new Labour government there started a fresh round of consultation with the Indian leaders how best to begin freedom in India. The poison of communalism had penetrated almost every limb of India and a surgical operation of partitioning of India became necessary. It was thus in peace and with the concurrence of Indian leaders that partition and freedom of India and Pakistan was achieved. However, the Muslim League did not realize that they had played into the hands of the imperialists by permanently alienating the Muslims of Muslim majority areas in Pakistan from the sizeable non-Muslim League minorities. Even before the partition actually took place ethnic cleansing was started in West Punjab and NWFP. Thousands of Hindus and Sikhs were butchered there. As a retaliation counter ethnic cleansing was begun in Bihar and East Punjab. Out of Indian states, the only state where there was relative peace was the state of Jammu and Kashmir with a Hindu Maharaja. Independent Pakistan with a nod, from British officer led Pakistan army and J. & K. militia, let Afghan and tribal raiders loose on the state from the west. To escape customary genocide indulged by the raiders, the Maharaja now with the support of the National Conference, the rebel political party of Muslims of the state acceded the state to the Indian Union and India decided to defend the state from the depredation by the raiders. This was the beginning of the so-called Kashmir question with a cease-fire line in the middle and all state territory to the west was quietly grabbed by Pakistan, which it has refused to vacate in spite of the U.N. resolution asking them to do so. Pakistan also did not give adequate recognition to the Bengali language, though the Bengali speaking people outnumbered others in Pakistan, and the Bengal public did not adopt Urdu. Pakistan tried to rule East Pakistan of Bengali speaking majority as a colony of West Pakistan, East Bengal had to wage a civil war for their independence from the stranglehold of the Punjabis of West Pakistan, which they won with the help of India. Thus the dream of imperialists of the division of Bengali speaking people was indirectly achieved. Bengal lies divided: West Bengal is a federating state of Indian Union and East Bengal is now free Bangladesh. West Bengal has for a long time a Communist party operating within the Indian Constitution. Bangladesh is alternating between the parliamentary majority now of Awami party that is secular and waged the freedom struggle against the communalists of Pakistan, and then of the Nationalist party of Zia and his widow which came to power after murdering the activists of the Awami League. This party without such admission is out to carry out ethnic cleansing of Bangladesh having accepted the bait of looting of the Hindus if forced to fly out of Bangladesh. The partition of Bengal has hit the nationalists of Bengal in two ways. The revolutionaries and communists of Bengal have been betrayed in East Bengal, while the efforts for Hindu-Muslim unity in Bengal and development of a composite Bengali culture have restricted scope only for West Bengal, which it will accomplish as a unit of the Indian union which swears by Hindu Muslim unity and equality in human rights of all its citizens. Voices of sanity are also heard in Bangladesh from its poets and thinkers.

Besides the scuttle through communal passions and rioting around the independence day in 1947, Bengal also paid heavily for its freedom in thought by the man-made famine after the Japanese occupation of Burma and INA incursion into India from the east. Millions of Bengalis became refugees or lost their lives in the holocaust. In 1948 whole of east India was full of Bengal beggars and refugees and these states nurtured by the sweat, blood and language of Bengal are now expressing their unhappiness with the Bengal presence in their midst. The conditions will improve with the development of industries in West Bengal and general prosperity of India given a couple of decades of peace for the enlightened policies of India to show results. The educated (and skilled in administration) Bengali is an asset for whole of South-east Asia. The shortsighted policy favouring natives everywhere should not debar wholesale stoppage to Bengali immigration, but their quota of immigration must be allowed on reciprocal basis as well as for the self-interest of other eastern states of India, Myanmar and Malaysia. An active SAARC can certainly be of help with projects jointly undertaken in various countries of South and South-East Asia. Advances in science and technology could be put in service for the rapid development of mineral wealth, hydroelectric potential and scenic beauty of the whole region from Malaysia in the East to West Bengal in the west.

9.3 Sri Ramakrishna and His Grasp of Hinduism

Ramakrishna was not a Vedist scholar but he was the teacher and guru of Vivekananda, the most celebrated exponent of Hinduism in the west. He was quite sure that Bhakti path can bring God close to human beings. The first task he set himself was to demonstrate the unity of God in whichever religion or god one puts one's trust. He was an ardent devotee of Kali and was appointed a pujari or ritual worshipper of the goddess in a temple at Calcutta. He went about doing the prescribed religious devotions to various deities including the Allah of the Muslims and claimed the pinnacle of success in each exercise. The disciples flocked to him and claim to be witness of his strange experiences. Vivekananda, then known as Narendranath, while a college student questioned him if he had seen God so that one could make own effort to meet Him. Shri Ramakrishna assured him that he had that fortune and could help Narendra also in his quest. Later Narendra is supposed to have had the religious trance that permits one to see the unity of the universe in God. Ramakrishna proved to the public at large the genuine religion they already have and have no need for any conversion to Islam or Christianity which had a field day since the supremacy of the Muslims and the British. He supported the Bengal reformers in believing in the solid foundation of the *Gita* for inter-religious coexistence and mutual respect. He was against superstition. He was all for religious reform and giving up of various kinds of senseless traditions and hankering for miracles. He was his own kind of traditionalist as well as a revolutionary.

The goal of renaissant Hinduism and of modern Indian society is of integration at a plane of equality rather than the old style of stratified stability which was already achieved in Bengal in the beginning of the 20th century. Hindus have never accepted the myth that Buddhism was a separate religion from Hinduism. From ancient times, the Buddha has been deified by the Hindus as an incarnation of Vishnu. His instruction is included in the Hindu idiom. At Nalanda, Vedism and Buddhism both were in the syllabus. Science and Technology is a great leveller and can serve integration of all communities and nations. Assured human rights are no longer the pipe dream of Mao or Marx waiting for dictatorship of one kind or the other that invariably brutalized first the leaders and then the people.

Islamic or Hindu Talibanization of Pakistan or India will never be attractive to free people of any country. Integration into a single civilized community deeper than mere coexistence and non-interference, that has been the tool employed by India for her continued existence and tiding over all kinds of disruption from inside or outside. Modern communications and technical developments mean more sophisticated efforts.

10

Bengal in Search of National Status

Medieval theocratic rule, oppression of Hindu subjects and neighbouring kingdoms could never make a nation. Democracy and equal rights of all citizens only could do that. This was the projected stance of the English company when it began to rule over certain area of Bengal after contending with and vanquishing the other European trading powers. They had extracted revenue collection rights from the Mughal and Afghan governors nominally appointed by the Mughal emperor at Delhi who was in such straits, that a mere hope of receiving his tribute from the regional power was enough for granting such rights. The court at Delhi or the court of the governor now practically a sovereign king at Murshidabad was riddled with corruption and inefficiency. The Muslims had established personal rule of kings or nawabs by strength of their armies and had lost all interest in the welfare of their subjects excepting for now and then a talented ruler who respected the country's expectations from rulers. They had not yet got to a proper system of succession. Every succession or replacement meant disaffection of certain powerful interests, rebellion or conspiracy. It took a generation of Englishmen to devote blood and toil to their Indian connection to win the subjects' confidence in the company rule. The productivity of Indian industries by Indian technology and Indian agriculture was enough to fill all European coffers engaged in buying Indian goods for sale at profit in Europe. In the beginning it was English and European gold and silver that came pouring into India. After they had purchased the loyalty of advisers of the king at Delhi and the Nawab at Murshidabad, they had forced the nawab to give them the authority of collecting the revenue in Bengal and Bihar. With this new source of wealth they could build a powerful military machine to tempt Indian rulers to seek their protection and support. The area under direct company rule expanded along with its administrative control and military threat to many neighbouring states. The Indian traders and money-lenders were already swarming to the side of the company. The Hindus were attracted by the European efficiency and regard of all subjects as equal before the company's law. They also soon realized that they were now the lower caste compared to Europeans and resolved to reform the Hindu society towards equal rights and humanist treatment of women which they had forgotten that it had started with ancient Hindu practice of their dharma. The European scholarship discovered the riches of the Indian classical literature and philosophy. The Indians learned it from the translation since earlier it was not disclosed by Brahmans to the uninitated. The East India Company was like a breath of fresh air after sustained destruction of Hindu institutions at the hands of conquering Muslims which had only slowly ceased since the rule of Akbar the Great at Delhi or Hussain Shah in Bengal. The Hindus in the company-run Bengal took full advantage of western education and became the junior partners in the administration of company rule from Calcutta. The Bengali influence spread all over India and particularly in the eastern region of India. Bengal started dreaming of a free united India of Bengal brand. Already a joint culture was emerging of Hindus and Muslims in Bengal. The philosophical underpinning was provided by Vaishnavism. Sri Ramakrishna and by rebellious Sufis. The European surrender to reason and their achievements in science and technology were continuous and not by the fits and starts of intuition and isolated genius. Indians, particularly the relatively free thinking Hindus took to modern science and technology as fish to water and now they are on the course to become more abundant in modern scientists, doctors and professionals ready to do their part in the modern development of the backward areas. Later the Indian freedom sounded the death-knell of all colonialism and the Indian experiments with capitalist production and the socialistic pattern of society is drawing respect of the developing world. Bengal has a great part to play to unite the aspirations of South Asia with East Asia thus strengthening peace and regard for the UN system in the future of mankind. The Bengali speaking Muslims of Bangladesh are sure to join Indian Muslims fully sharing Indian freedom for regenerating respect of human rights in the Muslim elite of the subcontinent and then of the other benighted Islamic states. Human future will be more certain by regard to reason as well as faith and prayers. There can be no theocratic hegemony over the whole world. The hope lies only in coexistence with spread of universal ethics a la Vivekananda and equality before law as is practically the basis of the present U.N. The U.N. still has some element of uncertainty visible in the form of permitted veto of certain countries and a divided Security Council with undue influence of super powers. The U.N. is basically bedeviled by poor financial resources and management. They could try Bengali skill as did the Englishmen of the 18th and 19th centuries who could build a unitary world empire on the shoulders of Bengali baboos and Bihari sepoys.

Various prerequisites of becoming a nation are adequately met by Bengal. People in a continuous area speak same language. They have a whole lot of classical and modern literature. They achieved considerable mutual understanding and respect between Hindus and Muslims. Important places of Hindu pilgrimage—Tribeni, Guptapara, Tarakewswar and Chinsura, had gatherings of masses at various fairs and festivals in which Bengalis of all faiths and levels participated. The great bathing festival in spring and *Sankranti* in winter were attended by all Bengalis. According to tradition Jafar Khan was a worshipper of Ganga. Even today Hindus swarm at the tomb of Jafar Khan which is a specimen of Muslim epigraphy. Mahesh who was miraculously favoured at Jagannath temple of Puri and the incident is mentioned in the legend of Satyanarayana retold at the popular Pooja of Bengal in which Hindus and Muslims both participate. Dara Ghazi of Tripura composed prayers in Sanskrit. The holy men of Hindu and Muslim faiths had considerable fellow feeling as has been evident also in the Punjab. The famines and floods affected the people without any distinction and they had to support each other. The unity and understanding between the Hindus and Muslims of Bengal was at its peak during the joint opposition to the division of Bengal in 1905. But unfortunately the unity was not harnessed to developing a Bengal national policy for the betterment of economic condition of the peasants. Even the communists could not get to grips with economic programmes. The cavalier treatment of Praja party leaders of East Bengal drove them at the crucial time of independence into the league fold and the communal passions went out of control in whole of Bengal.

Bengali nationalism might in future drive Bangladesh to seek closer ties with India. The small states of Eastern India will soon appreciate the past contribution of Bengal to their culture and development and would welcome select immigration of managers and technologists of Bengal. The atmosphere of cross border kinship will emerge through the works of neo-secularists of East and West Bengal. The non-official Netaji fairs will attract communists and nationalists alike and infuse new spirit into SAARC, language of culture besides English will be the Bengali language.

Mrs. Gandhi also wanted a distinct Bangladesh nation both Muslim and secular which could assist India as well as other countries of South Asia to cooperate in common aims for the region as well as the whole world including Pakistan.

11

Hindu Muslim Unity

The agenda of all Indian patriots and saints has been Hindu Muslim unity and co-existence of all faiths. In Indian states there was no oppression of Muslims when the prince was a Hindu and *vice versa*. The petty kings waged wars among themselves for the expansion of their kingdoms or reacted to any conspiracies threatening their despotic rule. Even the Delhi Sultans suppressed any growing threat to their power and usually their quarrel was with Muslim bigwigs who might be conspiring. The Hindus often were raised to high and responsible posts both civil and military. The armies on the march rarely vented their spleen on the common people whatever their religion. Hindus and Muslims were living together in the villages and cooperated with each other in the struggle for existence. The peasants and labour did not choose their clients or employers on the basis of religion. The artisans served all for remunerative work. Muslims worshipped unmolested in their mosques and the Hindus worshipped their idols. The fairs and festivals were jointly celebrated. The seeds of discord were assiduously scattered by the British imperialists after they had witnessed the united strength of Hindus and Muslims in the first war of independence when they could suppress the mutiny of their Indian mercenaries, or further after the annulment of the partition of Bengal in 1911. The imposition of communal electorates after staging petitions from the Muslims or the *dalits* was the start of the common people and upstart leaders identifying themselves with their communal labels. Upto 1933 people gave charity to all irrespective of Hindu or Muslim label of the donor or the recipient but after that time one could see differentiation in the distribution even of charity. I recall a Haji Sahib of Lahore in 1935 giving one paisa each to a Hindu Beggar and two paisa each to Muslim urchin who stood in the line of beggars every Friday at his shop selling spectacles and frames. Unfortunately when Indian prayers included a plea for everyone's welfare the Muslim prayed only for a Muslim's welfare. The legacy of Hindu-Buddhist, Zoroastrian or Christian thinking was not lost in West Asia even when their institutions were smashed by the barbarians of northern regions or later by the Arab-Iranian combine. Somewhat organized memory stayed on in the form of the syncritical Manicheism spread from Iran to Himachal Pradesh of India, the traces were apparent in the form of Kafiristan of northern Afghanistan or the folk religion of Himachal summarized in their chant "Mani Padme Hum" proclaiming the greatness of Mani who was otherwise quite forgotten under layers of popular Hindu-Buddhism. The spirit lingered on even when, nominally, all embraced Islam. This was seen in the Muslim Yoga or the intellectual devotional stance of the Sufis. The spiritualism of the Sufis was indistinguishable from the spiritualism of the Bhakti movement spreading in India from ancient times and having a new life from Babar's time when Guru Nanak sang the love of God into the hearts of the Punjabis. When the Muslim kingdoms were expanding at the cost of Hindu kingdoms in India, there was complete fellowship of mystics of the two faiths. The Hindu yogis still ranged nonchalantly in Islamic lands and the Sufi takyas were frequented by the Hindu peasantry. The ancient Guru-Chela *parampara* had spread concerning the takya-nishins who excited the same devotion as the Indian (Hindu-Buddhist and Jain) monks. This was particularly visible in northern U.P. and Bihar and Bengal. The popular Hindu-Muslim divide in India was created only in the inter-war period of early twentieth century by the imperialists when they cleverly imposed religious label based voting in place of straight human based democracy. The entire struggle of the Indian nationalism was not only with imperialism and colonialism but also with parochialism and religious compartmentalism, a parody of thoroughly discredited Hindu casteism. I recall the beginnings of Hindus keeping aloof from Muslims after the imposition of separate electorates and the beginnings of Hindu-Muslim social distance in the thirties of the twentieth century. In India religion ought not to be determining the political and social order. The ancient coexistence of all kinds of religious philosophies and their contention should have continued. Traditionally the Indians provided stage for intellectual contention in their six-yearly Kumbh fairs at holy places like Haridwar, Prayag, and Pushkar or many other sites along the Ganges also frequented by the Muslim preachers in the early centuries of Islam in India. Indian populace had always acclaimed new philosophies that appealed to them and found idolaterous holiness in ascetics or in holy relics first of Buddhist saints and later in the tombs and samadhis of qalandars and yogis or popular bhaktas.

Sufis though hounded out of their countries of origin were welcome in Central Asia and from there they would saunter into India as welcome spreaders of Islam in the border lands like northern and eastern India where they displayed the mysticism and love relationship of God with mankind. There was fraternal relationship between the Sufi saints and the Sikh gurus as well as the Vaishnava preachers and poets of Bengal. Unfortunately the Sikhs, a truly secular Bhakti group fell foul of the imperial Mughals particularly the Mughal-Afghan combination still concerned with the despotic empire of the Afghans or the Mughals in the Punjab and were subjected to untold cruelties but they weathered all storms till liberating themselves in the guise of Ranjit Singh's kingdom of the Punjab. In Bengal Afghan kings were in opposition to Mughal kings or governors which allowed the common people to continue to grow in natural relationship of Hindus and neo-Muslims. Bengal had also the good fortune of now and then their own Akbar like secular kings and Bengal could develop in relative peace and joint efforts of Hindu and Muslim poets, a vibrant Bengali literature that freely dealt with popular worship of rural and tribal deities. Over and above all this, the peculiar mixture of Afghan, Mughal, and Rajput power helped in the God sent Vaishnava movement guided by Chaitanya and his band of activists. Chaitanya also invented mass contact through popular singing processions including women and composed of all classes and religious labels in Bengal. The movement got support from professional musicians like the Bauls and energetic Bhaktas belonging to the Santal and other tribes of Bengal and Bihar. The neighbouring shrines to Jagannath at Puri and Ganges at Ganga Sagar provided the ever new crowds for Bengal style of inter-religious activity.

The Sufis and their way of thinking helped fellowship and commence between Hindus and Muslims. Hazrat Nizam-ud-din Aulia and his disciple Amir Khusro the famous Muslim poet using popular Hindi sided with the common people against all high-handedness of the Afghan court. In Akbar, the true secular emperor of India, Hinduism and Islam coexisted in equal measure. His heart had room also for the good points of Christianity and Jainism. By the close of the 17th century the country was consolidating Hindu and Muslim united living in the villages and the cities of India. They prayed freely according to their lights and celebrated their festivals together. Thursday the sacred day to the Sufis and Pirs of Islam saw the Hindus and Muslims gathering together at the takyas and the dargahs and sharing the sweets distributed by the pious to all in sight. It is interesting to see this even today at the dargah in Vasant Kunj where apart from Thursday gathering, the Hindus throng to celebrate the festivals of Holi and Diwali in place of going to distinctive temples which are few kilometres away. Hanuman, the god sacred to the Hindus and the rural folk gets a gesture of reverence from all users of the highway or from Indians of all castes and creeds. The tide of Indianness was turned when the lust for power drove Aurangzeb to play into the hands of fanatic mullahs who had helped him malign Dara the true heir of Shah Jahan as a non-Muslim because he was a scholar of Sanskrit and trained to govern the land of the Hindus and Muslims. He was adept in philosophy and mythology of the Indian religions. Aurangzeb was only a despot trying to usurp the title of Emperor of Hindustan. He is however venerated as a great Muslim hero by the fanatics among the Muslims of India and Pakistan, even when he trampled over the rights of others and was guilty of murdering his brothers and imprisoning his father. He started digging the grave of Muslim political power by senseless harshness to rebellious subjects particularly in the Punjab and Maharashtra. Aurangzeb continued to hold on to the empire in Bengal even though his advisers summed up the independent thinking of Bengal by holding Bengal to be hell embellished with food for the hungry and jewels for the Nabobs of Delhi and Calcutta. For the sake of his own despotic rule he continued to give high posts both civil and military to Hindus. His field commander was Raja Jaswant Singh, a Rajput, against the rebellious Sivaji, the Maratha chieftain, but his suspicious nature overcame his wisdom when against the advice of Raja Jaswant Singh, he mistreated the most important prisoner brought before him. However it is a canard against the Mughal organization to say that there was cruelty for the common people Hindus or Muslims in Aurangzeb's days. In fact the despotic empires of the Mughals or the East India Company did not disturb unduly the Hindus or the Muslims. They wanted only peace and support for the despot all over the country. The real drawback was that by the attempted non-interference they allowed the religion of India to go down hill. The superstitions became worse and the stage was set for the charlatans to mix with the truly spiritual guides and spread the misdirected hold of miracles and magic which completely overshadowed the tenets of Hinduism, Islam and Buddhism. Religion was saved by Vaishnavism in Bengal and Sikhism in the Punjab. On the other hand, Muslim fanaticism was fuelled by the British during the interval between the two great wars in order to prolong the life of the empire. They almost succeeded but for the intense jealousy they had created all over the world and later wisely shed colonialism under the benign influence of rebellious Gandhi and the arch rebel Netaji. The imperial policy of Britain even pitted the Sikhs against the parent faith of the Hindus. The Sikhs had already proven themselves on the side of the British in the storming of Delhi from the Punjab side during the sepoy mutiny. The Sikhs now have been brain-washed to the extent that they like to claim that Sikhism is a distinct revealed religion and that they were not Hindus, while their scriptures, worship, love of the preceptor and devotion to God is exemplary among all variety of Hindu Bhaktas. A Sikh when asked in England, if he was an Indian or a Pakistani, replied that he was a Sikh and allowed the interlocutor to remain in suspense. The Sikh Gurus had proclaimed that both Hindus and Musalmans were the children of one God. The Bengali folk had a peculiar solution for multiplicity of gods. They had a distinctive Hindu, or Muslim name for the same god or God. The Ganges there was the holy river for all. Many a tomb or memorial stone had worshippers from all faiths. The Bengal culture had crossed the various stages : Hindu, Buddhist, Jain or Muslim without surrendering to oblivion their past faiths. All faiths including the tribal ones co-exist even now. The common folk continue to worship many mother goddesses (calling them by Hindu or Muslim names when they wish prosperity in their fields and good health or their children escape from ailments.

Bengal provided two major instances of unity in India under the old dispensation. First was the occasion when Mangal Pandey, a mercenary of the British Indian army preferred to die than agree to use the obnoxious cartridges as ordered in 1857, thus setting the sepoys on the road to mutiny and India on the path of disobedience to colonial orders and later to the ordinance raj. The second one was the victory of united Bengal when the British were forced to undo the partition of Bengal in 1911. Imagine the reactionary slide from that day to 1947 when the partition of India was sought by Indians through the major political parties of Muslims and of Indians. This happened by the astute power play of the British. League theorized about a democratic Muslim homeland where the populace of religious majority or minority would enjoy full democratic rights. The Congress leadership considered them to be elected potential rulers of India including NWFP, Sind, Punjab and Baluchistan. While on the ground the Muslim masses had been goaded by the mullahs to rapine, loot and drive away the minority Hindus and Sikhs from the League's proposed Pakistan and the minorities would excite their counterpart Hindus and Sikhs in India notably in the Punjab, Bihar and around Delhi to retaliate in spite of the long training in non-violence and the importance of Hindu-Muslim solidarity instilled by Gandhi and Nehru. The communists had uncritically played into the hands of the British allies of Russia in the war against the fascists. Now that both India and Pakistan are no longer under the heel of the British, they still continue to be the victims and silent approvers of the divide and rule policy of the western imperialism in the form of preferential arms aid to India or Pakistan. The Indian caste system never transgressed to political level from the level of social inequity. While the caste system is being shorn of any vestiges of political and social upmanship, the leaders of communalism and regionalism are bent on spreading communal and regional hatreds all over India. They have succumbed to the communist doctrine of communal and regional nationalism. There is an urgent need of reversion to inter-religious and regional unity. The slogans of divisions of states and the communal label based division of government services and development funds have to be buried deep beyond resurrection. The policy outline has been provided by the requirement of total and continuous revolution by J.P. and unadulterated meritocracy by Netaji along with special educational and training facilities for the *Dalits* so that they can quickly stand up and be counted as equals.

The Indian hopes are now centred on the forces that may usher Unity in India where Hindu Muslim unity is the first step. Bengal is likely to lead the way. Bengal has repeatedly elected communist believers in equal democratic and economic rights of all human-beings. Now the time is ripe for the communists to embrace the wisdom and patriotism of Netaji as the most enlightened son of Bengal. The past collaboration between the communists and the imperialists on the doctrine of multiplicity of nationalisms in a nation state should now remain only an archival material and a freak of destiny. Bhadraloks in both East and West Bengals could cooperate in the uplift of all SAARC countries and institutions led by the policies of Gandhi and Nehru which are valid for all humanity like the moral life. Good deeds are basic to all religions and selfish exploitation of others is not a good deed. Secularism is an important aspect of New Mahayana, the *mantram* of coexistence. Hinduism is the religion of humanism and Islam, the religion of peace. The un-Islamic requirement of current Muslim leadership that for peace and cooperation, the whole world has first to be converted to Islam is not a Koranic injunction. The hand of friendship has to be extended to all without considerations of religion, region, race or sex. Indianness means peaceful coexistence in mutual rapport of all.

From every angle there is a demand for Hindu-Muslim unity. Only a new D'Rozarios from Bengal can bring this about as a necessary condition of modernization in all SAARC countries. The new breed of Ulema from East and West Bengal is sure to lead the way for the Muslims of the world for life in truly democratic multi-religious states.

11.1 Promotion of Unity

A cue can be taken from the social scene before modernization set in by the efforts of Bengal intellectuals. The mullah at the mosque provided leadership to the rural folk. The state must ensure proper training of the mullah and educate the rural population. Secularists should be placed in positions of influence that ensure self-censure to the media towards appreciation of various religions and deny the airing of rumors and running down of various forms of worship.

Akbar had understood the true nature of Hindu idolatory. Staunch Muslims in India should be taught this true nature of Hindu worship of idols. Hindu idolatory is just a form of worship and prayer. The communal riots start from trivia like the playing of music near mosques or throwing of Holi colour on a Muslim or quarrel among playing children. Such trivia can be recognized as such only when the grown up adults begin to lead a life of trust in their neighbours. The significance of Hindu formula to regard everyone as a civilized person should be taught to children in school. Cow slaughter, so long as it is not legally barred must be permitted to licensed butchers or meat making and packaging factories under medical and hygienic control regulations. The slaughter by individuals cannot be publicly carried out as it offends the religious susceptibility of many. Similar sensible decisions should control sale and partaking of pork. The Indians value the friendship of Muslims and must not offend their religious susceptibilities by public display of slaughtering pigs for food. It must however be widely distinguished that when Hindus do not eat beef, the reason is for the sanctity attached to the cow as well as the primary concern for adequate milk production and availability of bullocks for the peasants both for tilling the land as well as yoking to the village carts. On the other hand, the Muslims will not use pig meat because they look down on pork as unclean and unfit for human consumption. Pork however is consumed by many people particularly the Chinese and the Europeans. Bacon making is a great industry in Spain. There are historical reasons for Jews to take offence with pork which was the sacred offering of Romans at their altars after they won victories over the Jews and other inhabitants of West Asia. The problem of music before mosque can easily be resolved by disallowing music making processions in the vicinity of mosques unless it its done by mutual agreement. All meditation has to be carried out in silence and quiet attention. Music is also an essential ingredient of group prayer in many religions, and also close to the heart of Sufis among Muslims and in temples and churches as well as gurdwaras. The problem of music cannot be stretched to the extent of killing of people and rioting against innocent people. All cases of offending music should be brought before the elders of the village or the town committee or a court and matter resolved through acceptance of apology or submission to a fine.

Another issue has come up since the demolition of Babri Masjid in Ayodhya of insistence on amends for historical oppression as seen from mosques standing on the neglected temple structure below. Such amends for ancient historical misdeeds only perpetuate hatred and ill will among loving neighbours. Punjab Hindus and Mussalmans had begun to live like friends and brothers just before the issue of Shahidganj gurdwara mosque bedevilled their relationship in Lahore and later too the situation got worse with the distorted freedom when religious majority rule was established in parody of a political majority in true democracy. The integration process should be held as priority issue not to be side-tracked by childish matters pertaining to antiquity. Personal law should be codified and adopted for the whole country giving due consideration to special inherited practices of various groups and judicial permission to make exceptions where enforcement will go against national integration. Various communities of India should vie with each other in finding the middle peaceful way in all such matters.

India is committed against terrorism but is dragging its feet in support of American military occupation of Iraq. This must reassure the Muslims of India that in international affairs India does not intend taking up position which is manifestly against the NAM ideology and the UN principles of equality in freedom of all nations. India used with vigour the tools of boycott and *swadeshi* for own political freedom but is totally against such measures against other communities by the communalists in the same country as this spells ultimately slavery of both communities to the machinations of the imperialists. Everyone in India has to learn the secular adage that community label has no significance for business or social relations. With time inter caste and inter-religious marriages will increase as has happened in all democratic countries. In India already such marriages are quite legal. A country imbibes strength from the joint celebration of festivals and national events. All important religious celebrations should be celebrated as national events like the New Year, Christmas, Dussehra and Id-ul-Fitr, Durga Pooja or Muharram, Guru Nanak's birthday or Buddha Jayanti etc. A secular minded Hindu, Muslim, Christian etc. welcomes the spirit of enquiry and activism regarding reform in own religion by anyone. In a free country with assured human rights to all, any efforts to curtail such rights of any particular group must be nipped in the bud. Religious gatherings and *satsangs* should multiply in the pattern set up by the Secular Life Society *sastangs* at Delhi for the last few years where the individuals meet in friendship and hold discussion on reforms and steps that forward national integration. Secular Life Society invites all Indian citizens to conduct or join such *satsangs* and bring about a vibrant atmosphere conducive to national integration based on mutual security and mutual advantage.

Large scale communal clashes have political origin. Shia-Sunni conflicts hark to the ancient political struggle of two factions trying to grab political power in ancient Islam. Such clashes in India of modern times are quite senseless. In Bengal of the earlier century Sunnis also mourned with the Shias, the sacrifice of Shia leaders at Karbala. The reformists should hold open debates, now-a-days on TV with traditionalists so that reform movement spreads on solid foundation of popular acceptance and sooner than later we have in India a common personal law. In India the proper names should be indistinguishable community or religion-wise as prevailed upto recent times in Indonesia. It will be ideal for all Hindu temples to allow all, even non-Hindus, to enter and have *darshan* as is already regular practice in Christian churches and Sikh gurdwaras. A better plan might be having a separate meditation room dedicated to the use of irregular visitors to the temple or the Parsi Agiari etc.

The nation should sit down and resolve to use the national religious calendar for purposes of national integration. There are innumerable poojas and celebrations in calendars of Indian religions. The celebration dates should be transferred to weekends or summer and winter school and business vacations. (The pious can continue private feasting and fasting on the priestly ordained days). This is important as we cannot cut down on the working days since India needs lots more working days than they can gather in the religious calendars. Scientific and secular approach should be strengthened in every meet. All Indians might become familiar with the lives of great religious leaders and leaders of science and humanity: thinkers and philosophers of the world. National festivals in memory of secular thinkers and poets like Farid, Nanak, Kabir, Nehru, and Gorakhnath should be organized. Tribal dances and festivals should be encouraged in primary schools.

Selected Bibliography

Abdus Salam, Maulvi, *Riazus Salatin:* A History of Bengal.
Ambasthya, B.P. (Ed.), *History of the Portuguese in Bengal.*
Ascoli, F.D., *Early Revenue History of Bengal.*
Battasali, N.K., *Coin and Chronology of the Early Independent Sultans of Bengal.*
Bose, Manindra Mohan, *Post-Chaitanya Ahajiya Cult of Bengal.*
Bengal Secretariat Book Depot, *The Hoogly Imambara.*
Chatterji, Nandlal, *Mir Qasim, Nawab of Bengal* (1760-1763).
Chowdhury, Ranbir Roy, *Glimpses of Old Calcutta.*
Ghosh, Binoy Jiban, *Revolt of 1905 in Bengal.*
Hunter, W.W., *Annals of Rural Bengal.*
Majumdar, R.C., *History of Bengal*, Vol. I, Vol. II, Vol. III.
Moinuddin Ahmed Khan, *Muslim Struggle for Freedom in Bengal.*
Paul, Promod Lal, *The Early History of Bengal.*
Poddar, Arabinda, *Renaissance in Bengal.*
Roy, Asin, *The Islamic Syncretistic Traditions in Bengal.*
Roy, Dr. B.K., *The Career and Achievements of Maharaja Nand Kumar of Bengal.*
Sarkar, Jadunath, *Bengal Nawabs.*
Sarkar, Sushobhan, *Bengal Renaissance.*
Saxena, V.K., *Partition of Bengal.*
Walsh, J.H. Tull, *History of Murshidabad District.*

Index